LEEDS UNITED'S 'ROLLS-ROYCE'

THE PAUL MADELEY STORY

LEEDS UNITED'S 'ROLLS-ROYCE'

THE PAUL MADELEY STORY

David Saffer

TEMPUS

To my wife Ann, who always has time for others.

First published 2003

Tempus Publishing Ltd
The Mill, Brimscombe Port
Stroud, Gloucestershire GL5 2QG
www.tempus-publishing.com

© David Saffer and Paul Madeley, 2003

The right of David Saffer to be identified as the Author
of this work has been asserted in accordance with the
Copyrights, Designs and Patents Act 1988.

British Library Cataloguing in Publication Data.
A catalogue record for this book is available from the British Library.

ISBN 0 7524 3071 8

Typesetting and origination by Tempus Publishing.
Printed in Great Britain by Midway Colour Print, Wiltshire.

CONTENTS

ACKNOWLEDGEMENTS

Grateful thanks go to the following people and organisations for their help with this publication: Jimmy Armfield, Mike Fisher at Yorkshire Post Newspapers Ltd; Tony Lazenby; James Howarth and Emma Jackson at Tempus Publishing Ltd.

Images for this publication have been supplied by Yorkshire Post Newspapers Ltd; Leeds United Football Club and Jack Hickes Photographers. Every effort has been made to identify the original source of other illustrations. For questions regarding copyright contact Tempus Publishing Ltd.

Both Paul and myself would finally like to thank statistician Gary Shepherd for producing all the career statistics for this book. His efforts are greatly appreciated.

PREFACE

BY PAUL MADELEY

During and since my football career, my nature has always been to keep a low profile so readers may well be asking why this book has been written at all. When David Saffer suggested it my initial reaction was to say 'No thank you'. However, I have never been one to make decisions in haste and my wife, Ann, and two sons, Jason and Nick, thought it would be a good idea to record the whole of my nineteen-year career. I had already seen David's excellent work – *The Life and Times of Mick Jones* and *Sniffer: The Life and Times of Allan Clarke,* and he convinced me that my story is of particular interest as I was at Leeds United almost from the very start of the Don Revie era.

Finally I agreed, and gave David the go-ahead after Ann suggested that my share of the proceeds could be given to a charity. We decided on the National Heart Research Fund – who supply funds for heart research projects and are based in Leeds.

I must give thanks to my late father who kept records and newspaper cuttings from my schooldays and early days at Leeds United and to Ann for continuing the trend into my professional career. All the information proved invaluable in collating this book. I was never very good at saving memorabilia and confess to being quite blasé about the success of the Leeds United team in the late 1960s and early '70s.

Looking back I think my attitude was born out of confidence in the team and each year I expected that we would be involved in the later stages of any competition that we played in. Consequently, it did not seem special but just the norm' for this to happen so I never bothered to save things to look back on. I only have one signed team photo and thankfully it has Billy's signature on it.

Many of the older Leeds United supporters will be aware that my nickname was 'Ed'. I can't quite remember how this came about but my middle name is Edward so I suppose someone at the club started calling me Ed in the very early days and it just stuck. Even today whenever I see any of my former colleagues I am greeted with 'Hello Ed. How are you doing?'

Years ago I was often referred to as 'Big Ed' and people on meeting me, who hadn't seen me in the flesh, so to speak, would comment that I looked much bigger on the park. I had to explain that lots of footballers were quite small and at Leeds United if you were taller than Billy and Johnny you were referred to as 'Big'. Hence, 'Big Norman', 'Big Dave', 'Big Joe', 'Big Gordon', and of course 'BIG Jack.'

I am pleased and delighted to have played for Leeds when I did – I think that during that era there was a good deal more honesty in the game. By that I mean that players stayed on their feet a bit more. Nowadays they seem to go to ground at the slightest opportunity, making life extremely difficult for referees who have to instantly decide whether the fall is legitimate or not. It's a very difficult job and they can easily be made to look foolish by the slow motion replays that are beamed around the country.

Finally, I would like to apologise to any former colleagues and staff who don't get a mention in this book. It does not mean that I hold you in any less esteem but just goes to prove that all those mistimed headers are probably affecting my memory.

Paul Madeley

INTRODUCTION

My earliest memories of Leeds United date back to 1968 when my grandfather took me to the club's victory parade through Leeds City Centre following their League Cup final victory against Arsenal. Though only seven at the time I still recall the excitement as the players, holding the trophy, passed us on their open top bus. A few months later I went to my first match when my father took me to see Leeds defeat the Hungarian giants Ferencvaros in the Fairs Cup final. I was hooked.

Leeds United was a major force in the game and a key member of the team was Paul Madeley. Paul had joined as an apprentice in 1962 before making his first-team bow in January 1964. By his retirement in 1980 he would be the sole survivor at the club from his debut game, and had joined Billy Bremner, Jack Charlton, Norman Hunter and Paul Reaney as the only players to make over 700 appearances.

Stylish, professional and totally dedicated, Paul Madeley was a manager's dream. Don Revie famously described him as a 'Rolls-Royce' of a footballer. Playing in every outfield position for Leeds, the media dubbed him 'Mr Versatile' – a prowess that earned him universal respect from opposing players and managers alike.

During 18 years at Leeds, Paul played his part as Revie's team competed at the highest level at home and in Europe, winning Division One, FA Cup, League Cup and Fairs Cup honours. He also appeared in European Cup, European Cup Winners Cup and two further FA Cup finals. The latter part of his Leeds career saw the club enter a transitional phase as Revie's legendary side broke up.

On the international stage, after controversially turning down the chance to play in the 1970 World Cup finals, Paul went on to win 24 caps playing alongside Bobby Moore, Bobby Charlton, Geoff Hurst and Gordon Banks. Arguably his most memorable appearance came in England's 5-0 win over Scotland at Hampden Park, before he experienced World Cup heartache against Poland. Competing against world stars like Franz Beckenbauer, Dino Zoff and Johann Cryuff, Paul never let England down.

It is as a Leeds United player though that he is best remembered, and in this profusely illustrated biography Paul recalls the great matches in which he played and the personalities of his era. I've been privileged that Paul has shared his memories with me and would like to thank all the individuals who have given their time, particularly Jimmy Armfield for providing the foreword.

A one-club player, Paul Madeley was a remarkable footballer and an all-time great at Leeds United.

Enjoy the memories.

David Saffer

FOREWORD

BY JIMMY ARMFIELD

I once described Paul Madeley as something of a Rolls-Royce – what I implied was someone who would purr along, never giving a problem, always reliable and possessing all the extras when needed. I stand by that as Paul, or 'Ed' as we used to call him, was a thoroughbred in every sense of the word – to use the well-used term ... a manager's dream. Always pleasant, clean in habit, not an ounce of malice in his body, Paul Madeley always gave me the opinion that he was simply content to be a professional footballer playing for his beloved Leeds United.

Of course, he was more than just a player. He was an international, and even more than that, he was a versatile star who could play (at the top level) in several positions producing the same quality of performance. At Leeds, in my early days as manager, he played in midfield, but when Norman Hunter left, Paul moved to the back and did a terrific job for the club.

Don Revie once assured me, 'all Paul wants to do is play in the team! You can pick the other 10 then put him in place where you have a selection problem – but no matter what, he has to be in the eleven!' That did happen a few times with me. I once played him in left midfield at Arsenal and he gave their right side of defence a torrid time, using his pace down the left touchline looking as though he had played on the left flank all his career. But that was 'Ed' – and more importantly he did it with a smile on his face. He never once grumbled to me in four years.

A one-club man, Paul once agreed terms for a new contract with me, and then signed blank forms with no payment details typed on them. At the time he wouldn't want to play anywhere else anyway, he expected to be happy with the terms and would sign right away. He did and off he went. Total trust, no cynicism, that was the relationship Paul and I had, so it is indeed a pleasure for me to write this foreword to his book.

To all Leeds fans I can assure you that Paul is a true loyalist and as a player was an example to all around him. The rest of the squad and the fans took to him because simply he was a model for others to try and emulate ... A real Rolls-Royce!

Chapter One

FOOTBALL CRAZY

1945-1960

Paul Madeley was born in Beeston, Leeds on 20 September 1944. The youngest of three boys, sport and football in particular dominated his early years.

Our home at 14 Dalton Grove was a stone's throw from Leeds United football ground. My eldest brother John was six years older than me, so I spent a lot of my early years playing with Michael, 18 months my senior. My parents, John and Gladys, encouraged all of us in everything we did. It was a really happy home.

My mother worked part-time as a dinner lady for an organisation connected to my school, which made meals for local schools throughout my schoolboy days, so she was able to follow my development as a footballer, which I really appreciated. She was a tremendous inspiration and supported both Michael and myself from the touchline offering words of encouragement. Unfortunately, she never saw me play in the first team at Leeds because she passed away in November 1963, just two months before I made my full debut, however, she did see me play for the reserves, so had a taste of the atmosphere at Elland Road. Fortunately my father was able to follow me through my entire professional career, before his death in July 1988. For many years he was a clerk with British Road Services before joining the family business on the clerical side.

I always looked forward to the summer holidays – for a number of years we went to Blackpool. The big treat was going to the circus on the last night; my favourite act was the famous clown Charlie Cairoli. Later we went to Ryhl and Filey, where there were all sorts of fun activities. Christmas time was also very exciting. The most memorable was when I was ten because we moved to a new house in Farrar Lane, Adel, the week before. Everything was new; it was fantastic.

Paul began his education at Cross Flatts Park Junior School in Beeston and from an early age made headlines alongside his brothers in local papers. The *Yorkshire Evening Post* reported in 1953:

Three boys who are giving commendable displays with the Cross Flatts (Beeston) teams in Leeds Schools FA games this season are the Madeley brothers – John (14), Michael (10) and Paul (9). John, captain of the senior team from centre-half, has been on the fringe of City honours all season. A natural ball player and a skilful inside-forward, he played against Don and Dearne in the third round of the English

John and Gladys Madeley on their wedding day.

The Madeley boys, Michael, John and Paul, 1947.

The Madeley boys with Dad and Aunt Lillian, *c.*1948.

Sprint King! Paul is the clear winner of this race whilst on holiday, *c*.1955.

Schools trophy, and has also played in five friendlies. Michael is centre forward in the school's outstanding junior side, and also played last year, when the team was undefeated. To date he has scored 18 goals, recently claiming 5 out of 10 against Lower Wortley. Paul was only 8 when the season started, but even so, he can hold his place at left-half in a side which aims at bettering last season's wonderful record. This gives Paul two more seasons as a junior. It would seem that the name Madeley is likely to crop up in Leeds City boy's sides for many seasons yet.

The manager of Cross Flatts school football team, following a tip-off from Paul's brothers, soon realised the youngest Madeley had talent. In an interview with the *Yorkshire Evening Post*, Mr Paul Jordan recalled Paul's school debut against Lower Wortley on a local 'rec'. 'I only saw Paul play for a couple of minutes before I realised he would be a first-class footballer. Paul had an outstanding game, and played very intelligently at left-half. He found no difficulty in filling a difficult role.'

The team remained undefeated for five years and was recognised as the best side in Leeds schoolboy soccer during the early 1950s. A member of the 'Champion of Champions' team for three years, his growing prominence led to him being featured in a local paper's 'Schoolboy Portrait'. The reporter's long-term speculation on his future prospects is particularly noteworthy.

Paul would have a strong claim to the title of *unluckiest schoolboy player of the season*. he played one game for Leeds City Schools FA team last season when only an Intermediate, and then played through the full programme of friendlies this

Pull! Paul's team are all smiles as they win this tug-of-war bout, *c*.1955.

Cross Flatts School Junior rugby team, 1955. Paul is on the back row fourth left.

Smiling schoolboy, c.1956.

season, only to be injured in the last one against Rotherham, in October. Paul hasn't played since, but is now training again, and hopes to turn out on Boxing Day in the schools shield semi-final *v.* Harehills at Oldfield Lane. He was captain of Cross Flatts Juniors and captain of the Leeds Junior side of that year which won the Clarke Cup at Scunthorpe. Paul's lucky thought is that he has yet another season of schoolboy soccer and a bright chance of the highest honours.

Paul moved to Parkside County Secondary Modern School aged eleven, where apart from being a budding footballer he was also a Leeds junior sprint champion. His sprint ability led to a hectic sports day, and there was also the small matter of rugby league and cricket...

Football was the major part of my childhood. Although my father ran a local amateur football team before I was born, in which several uncles played, we were not a family with a sporting history. However, it was the classic thing in those days, all the boys in the area played football. Our terraced house was on a very narrow street, the houses acted as the sides of the pitch and the grates identified the goals. We played from morning till night, and if we didn't have a full-size ball we'd use a tin can or tennis ball.

In the summer, after school we'd go to the local park and play for hours. There was always a game on. Our coats were the goals and the teams could be anything, 20 even 30-a-side would be the norm. It was great fun and it certainly improved your skills. My parents were very supportive because it was healthy exercise and it kept us from wandering the streets.

My team was naturally Leeds United. We used to walk to the ground from my house and stood in the Boys enclosure next to the Kop. I recall them playing in Division Two before winning

15

Boyhood heroes … Leeds United, 1956/57. From left to right, back row: Kerfoot, Ripley, Dunn, Wood, Hair, Charlton. Front row: Meek, Nightingale, Charles, Brook, Overfield.

promotion at the end of the 1955/56 season. The star of the first team was of course John Charles, and if ever there was such a thing as a one-man team, it was then. He was so strong in the air and had a really powerful shot. It didn't matter whether he played at centre-half or centre forward, John stood out. After he left in 1957 for Juventus the team began to struggle. He was a phenomenal player. I also remember Billy Bremner in his early days at the club in the late '50s. Billy never stopped running, you could see that he had talent.

I wasn't too concerned about failing my eleven-plus because Parkside had only just opened and it was well known for its sports facilities. The school team won lots of honours in football throughout my years in the team, but I also played at centre for the rugby teams from under-12 to under-15 level and cricket because I could bowl a bit. Although we played on grass, amazingly the wicket was concrete!

My speed was always an asset and saved me playing in the scrum at rugby! More important though I was able to represent the school at Roundhay Park in the 'Hill 60' races. The semi-finals took place during the week, before the finals in front of spectators at the weekend. I first took part when I was nine, and much to my surprise won. I remained unbeaten for four years until a flyer called Paul Reaney beat me in the heats – but I got my revenge in the final!

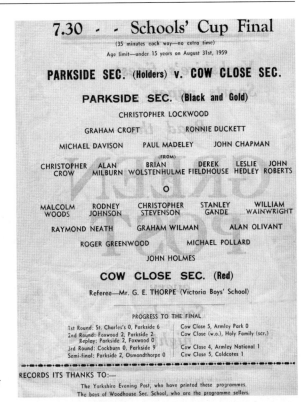

7.30 · · Schools' Cup Final

(35 minutes each way—no extra time)

Age limit—under 15 years on August 31st, 1959

PARKSIDE SEC. (Holders) v. COW CLOSE SEC.

PARKSIDE SEC. (Black and Gold)

CHRISTOPHER LOCKWOOD

GRAHAM CROFT   RONNIE DUCKETT

MICHAEL DAVISON   PAUL MADELEY   JOHN CHAPMAN

(FROM)

CHRISTOPHER   ALAN   BRIAN   DEREK   LESLIE   JOHN
CROW   MILBURN   WOLSTENHULME   FIELDHOUSE   HEDLEY   ROBERTS

O

MALCOLM   RODNEY   CHRISTOPHER   STANLEY   WILLIAM
WOODS   JOHNSON   STEVENSON   GANDE   WAINWRIGHT

RAYMOND NEATH   GRAHAM WILMAN   ALAN OLIVANT

ROGER GREENWOOD   MICHAEL POLLARD

JOHN HOLMES

COW CLOSE SEC. (Red)

Referee—Mr. G. E. THORPE (Victoria Boys' School)

PROGRESS TO THE FINAL

1st Round: St. Charles's 0, Parkside 6	Cow Close 5, Armley Park 0
2nd Round: Foxwood 2, Parkside 2	Cow Close (w.o.), Holy Family (scr.)
Replay: Parkside 2, Foxwood 0	
3rd Round: Cockburn 0, Parkside 9	Cow Close 4, Armley National 1
Semi-final: Parkside 2, Osmondthorpe 0	Cow Close 5, Coldcotes 1

RECORDS ITS THANKS TO:—

The Yorkshire Evening Post, who have printed these programmes.

The boys of Woodhouse Sec. School, who are the programme sellers.

Up for the Cup! Parkside defend their School's Cup final, 1959.

We won the Cup! Parkside show off their trophies, 1959. Paul is seated on the second row fourth left.

On the football field Paul was progressing and soon gained recognition with Leeds City boys, Yorkshire boys and North of England boys at under–15 level.

Both my brothers had represented Leeds City boys. Michael was a regular when I joined him in the under-15 team. I played two seasons at centre-half alongside Paul Reaney, a budding centre forward at the time, Kevin Hector, Rod Johnson and Alan Milburn. We played in the Yorkshire Schoolboys Cup and English Schools Cup but failed to progress to the latter stages. Rod went on to play a few games for Leeds during the '60s whilst Kevin had a lot of success at Derby County. One of my best friends was Alan, a descendent of Newcastle United's legendary striker Jackie Milburn and a nephew of George Milburn, who played for Leeds United. He was quite a player and a tremendous schoolboy footballer. He had a number of trials, but didn't really progress, which was a pity because he had talent.

Yorkshire boys were also quite a formidable outfit. I recall one match in particular when we beat Lancashire boys 4-0 at Barnsley; we were naturally pleased with ourselves because of the county rivalry. In our side were Len Badger and Frank Casper. Both went on to enjoy League careers at Sheffield United and Burnley respectively.

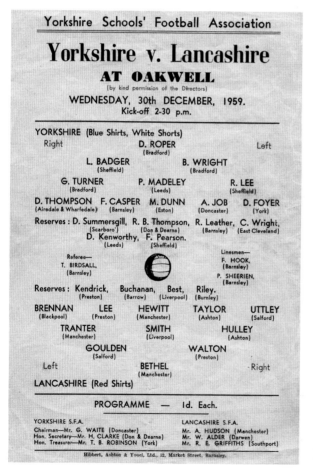

Battle of the Roses ... and Yorkshire won 4-0!

I was clearly progressing, because Manchester City and Arsenal offered me trials, but my parents were keen for me to get some qualifications in case I didn't make it, so I turned both teams down. I was still playing regularly for the school on Saturday mornings and turned out in the afternoons with Middleton Parkside's youth team. Before long it was time to leave school and I was pleased that I'd passed O-levels in English Language, Maths, Art, Woodwork and Technical Drawing.

Prior to an FA County Championship match, West Riding *v.* Sheffield & Hallamshire, the *Green* was pleased to note that Paul Madeley had been included at right-half. The reporter commented, 'Madeley must have caught the selectors eye even last season, for at that time he was the most outstanding player in Leeds schoolboy football. He was captain of both the Leeds and Yorkshire County Boys' teams as well as having a number of international trials.'

Before a West Riding County Minor Cup match for Leeds and District FA against Halifax, Terry Lofthouse of the *Yorkshire Evening Post* praised the number of local teams who had quality players. He went on to single out one player in particular. 'One who is a *must* from the start is that brilliant South Leeds right-half Paul Madeley, who is expected to provide the driving power from the rearguard. Madeley, has of course received County honours this season.' Among Paul's teammates in the team were Rod Johnson and Paul Reaney of Middleton Parkside.

Following a 'North' trail match at Barnsley, local reporter Lionel Jackson wrote, 'Two boys stood out – Paul Madeley (Leeds) and David Pleat (Nottingham). Madeley gave a polished display at centre-half for the North, who beat North Midlands 3-1. Following the game the North's English Schools selectors chose their team to face the South at Kettering. Both Madeley and Pleat made the XI.'

Paul's performances were gaining more and more recognition. Captain of Leeds City Boys, Yorkshire and North of England, though not his school team, after playing for both 'the Rest' and England in a trial match, Paul became the first Leeds boy since the war to be selected for a schoolboy international squad. However, despite call-ups for games against Ireland (twice), Scotland and France, Paul failed to make the final XI, so missed out on being awarded an England schoolboy cap.

It did disappoint me, but at least I was getting recognition. Only two players in our team made the grade at the top, Ron Harris (Chelsea) and Len Badger (Sheffield United), although Barry Fry, who played inside right, went on to successfully manage a number of clubs in the lower leagues.

As he prepared for his GCE's, one local paper summed up his schoolboy career. 'He will remember his school days with pride for his school last year won many honours. They were unbeaten in the league, unbeaten in the cup, and not a goal conceded all season.'

Publicity aside, Paul's parents were keen for their son to get a job with a future ...

I was offered a job at an insurance broker, Fipps Charnley Ltd in September 1961. They were situated near all the banks in the city centre, but I hated it. Football-wise I joined Farsley Celtic.

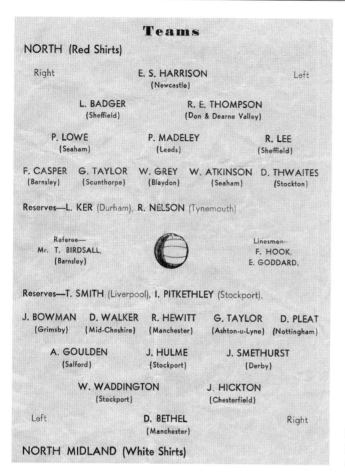

Teams

NORTH (Red Shirts)

Right   E. S. HARRISON   Left
(Newcastle)

L. BADGER   R. E. THOMPSON
(Sheffield)   (Don & Dearne Valley)

P. LOWE   P. MADELEY   R. LEE
(Seaham)   (Leeds)   (Sheffield)

F. CASPER   G. TAYLOR   W. GREY   W. ATKINSON   D. THWAITES
(Barnsley)   (Scunthorpe)   (Blaydon)   (Seaham)   (Stockton)

Reserves—L. KER (Durham), R. NELSON (Tynemouth)

Referee—   Linesmen—
Mr. T. BIRDSALL,   F. HOOK,
(Barnsley)   E. GODDARD.

Reserves—T. SMITH (Liverpool), I. PITKETHLEY (Stockport).

J. BOWMAN   D. WALKER   R. HEWITT   G. TAYLOR   D. PLEAT
(Grimsby)   (Mid-Cheshire)   (Manchester)   (Ashton-u-Lyne)   (Nottingham)

A. GOULDEN   J. HULME   J. SMETHURST
(Salford)   (Stockport)   (Derby)

W. WADDINGTON   J. HICKTON
(Stockport)   (Chesterfield)

Left   D. BETHEL   Right
(Manchester)

NORTH MIDLAND (White Shirts)

Step one … English Schools International 'northern' trial match.

Paul made his debut along with brother Michael against Scarborough in the Yorkshire League and immediately received promising reviews in the *Green Post*. Snippets continued to appear and Tom Hardwick in the *Green Post* exclusively predicted his future in December 1961.

> Farsley Celtic have a lot of leeway to make up if they are to have any say in the honours this time. The villagers will want their strongest possible team in the fight ahead, and it is a pity that they seem likely to lose Paul, the younger brother of the two talented Madeley brothers. Right-half Paul has been attracting a great deal of attention from League clubs in the short time he has spent in the Farsley first team, and Leeds United have frequently had scouts watching him. Now I understand that there is a distinct possibility of his joining the Elland Road ground staff and taking professional football as a career. It could well be that today's appearance in the home game against Norton Woodseats was his last in Farsley colours.

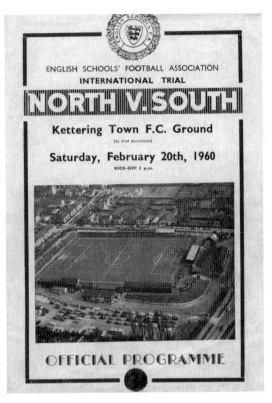

Right: Step two ... North *v.* South Trial.

Below: Step three ... English Schools International 'national' trial match.

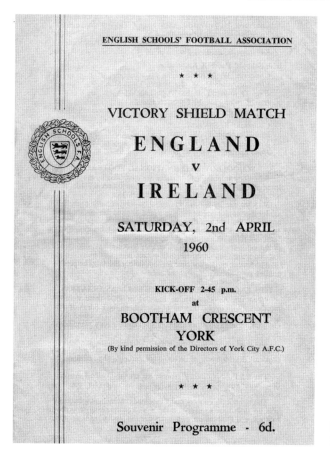

ENGLISH SCHOOLS' FOOTBALL ASSOCIATION

★ ★ ★

VICTORY SHIELD MATCH

ENGLAND

v

IRELAND

SATURDAY, 2nd APRIL
1960

KICK-OFF 2-45 p.m.
at
BOOTHAM CRESCENT
YORK
(By kind permission of the Directors of York City A.F.C.)

★ ★ ★

Souvenir Programme - 6d.

Final Step ... English Schools
International match.

Within a week Paul had signed for Leeds. The *Green Post* reported: 'It was a bitter blow for Farsley Celtic when young Paul Madeley left them to join Leeds United's ground staff, but there should be a nice bit of compensation for the villagers. The Elland Road club have promised Farsley a very agreeable sum of money if the pivot starlet turns professional for them and the youngster is playing so well that it seems to be only a question of time.'

I only played four months with Farsley Celtic before Leeds United spotted me, because somehow I got selected to play for a Leeds City under-18 team against Leeds United juniors on their training pitch. I must have impressed Don Revie because he came round to my house afterwards and sold the club to me. Even though Leeds may not have been the most fashionable team around, Don had so many ideas. He explained that he was developing the youth set up and wanted me to be part of his plans. Don was determined to only bring the best players to the club. It didn't take me long to agree to join the ground staff as an apprentice professional. I was determined to succeed and had just a single objective, to be offered a professional contract.

Chapter Two

MAKING THE GRADE

1962-1966

Paul's first day at Leeds United was 2 January 1962. The *Green Post* reported that one of his first jobs was to help 'snow-clearing operations' in readiness for the cup game with Derby County. Paul was well aware that only a few apprentices made it to the very top of the sport, but this local lad was determined to make an impression.

> *There were a number of promising youngsters at the club on the ground staff. Future stars like Norman Hunter, Paul Reaney, Gary Sprake and Terry Cooper were already playing in the junior and reserve teams. Although I was thrilled to be able to begin a career as a professional footballer, life was far from glamorous.*
>
> *We arrived at 9 a.m. and our jobs would be designated before we did any training. Duties included collecting the dirty kit from the changing rooms, cleaning the players' boots, setting out the strips, sweeping the terraces or helping the groundsman; it was not all about playing football. The professionals arrived at 10 a.m. and changed for training, which was taken by Don Revie, Les Cocker, Bob English and Syd Owen. When I signed for Leeds, having success in terms of trophies didn't cross my mind. At the time Leeds was a struggling Division Two outfit, but that didn't matter. I was at a professional club and my goals were simple, gain a professional contract and make the first XI.*

Paul's performances won recognition to the England Youth team. After winning caps against Scotland and Wales, Paul played in an international tournament in Rumania.

> *It was a tremendous experience and it was certainly useful trying to combat the different tactics that European players adopted. Results-wise it was not a success though, because we were well beaten in our games.*

On his return Terry Lofthouse, *Yorkshire Post*, featured Leeds United's rising star.

Most aspiring young soccer players have high hopes of one day playing in the Football League, but the percentage of those who make the top grade is very small. If sheer determination counts for anything, however, 17-year-old Paul Madeley of Adel in Leeds is destined to make a name for himself in football ... Some people might say that with his GCE in five subjects behind him, Paul would have been wiser to have chosen a much more secure way of life. But this 'giant' is determined to get to the top in football.

Welcome to Leeds United! Paul helps Syd Owen with 'snow-clearing operations' on his first day at the club.

Whilst Paul learned his trade, the first team was struggling and it looked odds-on they would be relegated, but Don Revie pulled a masterstroke when he signed Bobby Collins.

I remember Bobby well. He had a fierce determination to win at all times and played a significant role in Leeds staying up that 1961/62 campaign. There were a few players going nowhere who were content to be in the reserve team; it was a way of life without too much pressure. They didn't have the driving ambition and were not prepared to work hard at it. I recall a player saying once before a game, 'Okay lads, the sooner we get out the quicker it will be over with.' It certainly wasn't a war cry to play well, and did not impress Bobby. He quickly changed that attitude!

Results began to improve rapidly as Don Revie, true to his plans, blooded his young stars. Leeds ended the 1962/63 campaign in a creditable fifth position with Gary Sprake, Paul Reaney and Norman Hunter establishing themselves in the first team alongside Billy Bremner, Jack Charlton, Willie Bell and Bobby Collins as Revie put together a side capable of challenging for promotion. During the close season, Eire international Johnny Giles arrived from FA Cup winners Manchester United to further strengthen the team. As for Paul Madeley, he achieved his first ambition, a professional contract.

I played in the youth team and soon got promoted to the reserves, in the main as a defender. I'd also seen my wages rise. Starting out on £7 10 shillings, Don had given me a pay rise to £12 before my first professional wage of £20 a week. Signing my first professional contract was a big step because it wasn't unusual for ground staff boys to be shown the door after a year. Obviously Don saw some potential in me, even though I didn't think I'd progressed very much. Fortunately he did and placed me on the retained list. I still recall Don coming over to me casually at the end of my first season and saying he'd be keeping me; I was absolutely delighted.

Leeds began the 1963/64 Division Two campaign as one of the favourites for promotion. They didn't disappoint. Revie's promising team quickly raced to the top of the league alongside Sunderland and Preston North End. It was clear that they had a real chance of returning to Division One. Paul was a fixture in the reserves alongside more young stars like Jimmy Greenhoff, Eddie Gray, Peter Lorimer and David Harvey, and was waiting for his first-team opportunity.

By January, Leeds were sitting at the top of the table, but suddenly Revie had an injury crisis looming. Jack Charlton had been sidelined since the beginning of November and would be out for a further few weeks. His replacement Freddie Goodwin had just broken a leg during a 1-0 win against Cardiff City in a third round FA Cup-tie. Paul Madeley was Leeds' third choice ...

Leeds were due to face Manchester City, and Revie was now forced to consider fielding their youngest defence ever with an average age of just 20 years and 10 months. Father of the defence was Willie Bell (26). Sprake (18), Reaney (19), Bremner (21) and Hunter (20) completed the six, whose aggregate age was 124 years 11 months. The first hint that Paul would play arrived when Don Revie called him up to train with the first team during the week. As the wide-eyed youngster sprinted with Bobby Collins, Billy Bremner, Ian Lawson and Albert Johanneson, he told a *Yorkshire Evening Post* reporter:

All the best from the club ... Paul wins England youth honours.

This is a thrill in itself. I never dreamed it would happen. If I get picked on Saturday it will be marvellous.

In an interview with Richard Ulyatt of the *Yorkshire Post* Don Revie confirmed his decision: 'I shall in all probability give young Paul Madeley a chance. After all, he has been making great strides at centre-half in the Central League side and on Saturday played powerfully in our 2-0 win at Old Trafford against Manchester United reserves. Paul has earned his chance. I've every confidence in him. He's very mobile, reads a game well and he's learning fast.'

The night before the game Paul told reporters:

I feel great at being selected. My only regret is that my mother will not be there to see my debut. It was her greatest ambition to see me play for the first team, but she died a few weeks ago. Mum was keen as mustard about football and did everything to help and encourage my career. This is a great club and I'm determined not to let them down; there's too much at stake.

Leeds won 1-0, thanks to a Don Weston strike two minutes into the second half. Reporters were impressed with Revie's youngsters if not the overall performance.

Richard Ulyatt, *Yorkshire Post*: 'The youngest defence Leeds United have ever fielded gained greatest satisfaction from this hard, often frustrating and sometimes clever match … Madeley gave little away and highlighted a sound display with an off-the-line clearance … Leeds could have won by seven goals, to stay at the top they will have to become more clinical.'

Eric Todd, *Guardian*: 'Leeds should have won more comfortably … Every time duty takes me to Elland Road I am reminded of the song about the railroad running through the middle of the house … Leeds on this showing are not ready for the First Division. The raw material is there; whether it would stand up to repeated hard wear is another matter. Collins of the twinkling feet and eyes, and the shrewd brain is an ideal mentor for Leeds's prolific kindergarten from which Madeley performed creditably on his first senior appearance. Nevertheless, Mr Revie should hasten to

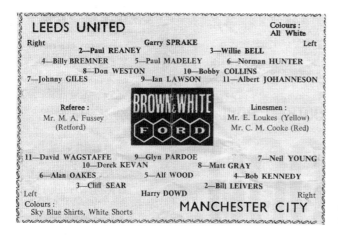

At last … Paul makes his first-team debut, 11 January 1964.

explain to his charges the considerable difference between enthusiasm and petulance. Younger players, and not only at Leeds, need strict discipline and probably less money until they have learned the value of both.'

Phil Brown, *Yorkshire Evening Post*: 'Leeds United can sigh again with relief at having beaten Manchester City, but their painfully faulty finishing kept their winning margin to the minimum. I still think United will go up mind you, but they bring your heart into your mouth too often to induce 100 per cent confidence. Young Madeley finished on the merit side at centre-half on debut. His positioning and anticipation went adrift sometimes, and understandably amid the tensions of his first and a vital match for United, but he grafted and never flinched.'

My father and brothers came to the game. I marked Glynn Pardoe, who bizarrely was also making his debut. I'd played against Glynn before for Yorkshire Boys. I did quite well, which I was really pleased about because this was the real thing.

With Charlton out for a month, Paul kept his place in the side against Swindon Town. Two goals down inside 14 minutes, Leeds were up against it, but the teams' never-say-die attitude claimed a 2-2 draw. Revie commented afterwards: 'I always ask for 100 per cent effort and thanks to the players we are always getting it. I thought our handicapped side did particularly well in both determination and football.' *Yorkshire Post's* correspondent thought young Madeley 'slogged away in the best United tradition.'

Next up for the youngster was a clash against the defending League Champions Everton in a fourth round FA Cup clash at Elland Road. Leeds looked as if they may cause an upset when Lawson gave them a first-half lead, but a twice taken penalty nine minutes from time saved the First Division side. Reporters praised Leeds.

Phil Brown, *Yorkshire Evening Post:* 'United were the liveliest underdogs you could imagine. Again the hour and the need produced the men... Madeley responded gallantly with the best game of his three so far. He is tuning in fast to the sharper needs of senior football, and of his courage there was no doubt at all.'

Eric Todd, *Guardian:* 'Leeds United gave Everton a good run for their considerable money. Everton may have had the stamp of class, but were in the end lucky to escape. Even their best friends could not fairly mention Leeds and class in the same breath, and I hasten to add there is nothing to be ashamed of in that. Miss Eliza Dolittle did all right for herself. Leeds appeared to be as overshadowed on the field as they were off it when the Everton party arrived in its new luxurious coach. Nevertheless, Leeds' backs and half-backs settled down and did a first-rate job, and young Madeley excelled himself against Young... Everton should have won and Leeds could have.'

Leeds lost the replay 2-0 but progress was being made.

Phil Brown, *Yorkshire Evening Post:* 'For a side stripped by injury of so much experience to give the League Champions a real fright was one more feat in United's exciting season... Madeley defied his youth and inexperience with a sound job at centre-half. Sooner or later he should 'arrive'.'

One area Leeds needed to reinforce was in attack. The team was creating chances, but too many were clearly being wasted. Revie acted by bringing in the former England international Alan Peacock. Making an immediate impact he scored on his debut in a 2-2 draw at Norwich City. With Charlton close to regaining his fitness, Paul deputised, as he did for his final appearance of the season in a 1-0 win against Scunthorpe United.

Of his run in the first team, Don Revie commented: 'He's done extremely well coming into the side at such a difficult time. One thing he has proved beyond all doubt is that he has the ideal temperament for the job.'

What I recall most about my debut and early games for Leeds was the noise of the crowd. It's amazing how much shouting goes on between players during a match, 'man on', 'square ball' and so on. I'd been warned about how hard it would be, but it's impossible to simulate crowd noise until you actually play a game, and it took me by surprise. When the crowd roared, you couldn't hear each other, but I soon got used to it.

It was such a different game going from amateur to professional in terms of speed on the ground, speed of thought and general sharpness. It took me quite some time to get there, and in some respects even when I made my debut I wasn't quite there. However, once I was at the right level, I made sure that I never lost it. I was delighted to have had a run in the side.

It was a youthful team with a few older heads in the side. Bobby Collins in particular was inspirational. Bobby was very talented, hard as nails and a terrific captain. Before a match he was really fired up and couldn't wait to get out onto the pitch. He also helped toughen me up, because it wasn't my natural game. On the training ground you could have a laugh and a joke, but I remember him on more than one occasion let me know he was around. There was no animosity, he looked at me and told me that's what I should be doing … get stuck in before they impose themselves on you.

As Paul continued his education in the reserves, Leeds powered towards the Championship, clinching promotion at Swansea before tying up the title at Charlton Athletic on the last day of the season. Don Revie's boys were back in the big time again. Following the team's promotion the *Yorkshire Evening Post* offered these prophetic words:

Leeds United have got out of the Second Division in time for the city's club to become the name it should be but never has been. It was club chairman Mr Harry Reynolds who advocated the appointment of Mr Don Revie, then only thirty four and the youngest manager in the League. Mr Revie has been the find of this generation as a manager. In his three years he has saved the club from relegation and won promotion. Mr Reynolds has stated that this is only the first step. The board wants Leeds United on the football map of Europe as well as the football map of Britain. The next few years should be interesting at Elland Road.

I wasn't with the first-team squad when we clinched promotion and the title, as I had a reserve game, but we were all naturally delighted because so many of us were at the beginning of our

Leeds United, 1964/65. From left to right, back row: Bell, Hunter, Reaney, Charlton, Greenhoff, Cooper. Middle row: Owen (coach), Peacock, Weston, Sprake, Revie (manager), Williamson, Madeley, Wright, English (physiotherapist). Front row: Bremner, Giles, Storrie, Collins (captain), Henderson, Weston, Johnson.

careers. Hopefully it would not be too long before I could take on the likes of Manchester United and Liverpool.

After a restful summer, the players got down to pre-season training.

It was really hard work, however there was a real buzz within the club. I quickly learned to stay fit throughout the summer by doing some roadwork, which made pre-season training easier.

Leeds surprised everyone during their inaugural campaign by almost clinching the 'double', missing out on goal average to Manchester United in the League and in extra-time at Wembley to Liverpool in the FA Cup final. Paul made a total of seven appearances and proved something of a lucky talisman, as Leeds defeated Stoke City, Burnley, Blackburn, Sunderland and Everton. The team's 2-0 win at Blackburn drew great reviews as Leeds came of age.

Derek Hodgson wrote: 'On a night raw enough to keep Wenceslas at home Leeds finished their merriest Christmas with a victory that makes them joint kings of the First Division. Live, lean Leeds were twice as nimble as Rovers on a heavily sanded, frost-bound pitch. They won for the reason that has become so familiar to First Division clubs. Leeds will do twice as much work in half as much time as almost any other team. Fifteen minutes from time the *Leeds Leeds Leeds* chant was ringing round Ewood Park along with a local improvisation *Bye Bye Blackburn*.'

Paul and Willie Bell stop a Burnley attack. Bell scored Leeds goal in a 1-0 win.

My top-flight debut was against Stoke City at full-back, and it went well. Winning against Blackburn took us to the top of the table, which surprised a lot of people. Performance-wise the pick was against Everton when the team was coming to the end of a great unbeaten run (18 games). Albert was on song, scoring two great goals.

Although I was only part of the squad, the commitment of us all was total and we surprised a lot of teams. I'd made a few appearances and was part of the Cup Final squad. I stayed at the team hotel, and it was all very exciting with it being the club's first FA Cup final, however, there were no substitutes in those days so I watched the game from the stands. The only bright moment was when Billy scored.

Leeds began the 1965/66 campaign in fine form. After coming on as a substitute at Tottenham, an injury to Willie Bell gave Paul a run in the side at left-back. Settling in immediately he surprised everyone, including himself, with a first goal for the club in a 3-3 draw with Leicester City. He went on to make 13 League appearances in all, mainly in defence.

Over the years I only scored a few goals, so I recall them all! Against Leicester, Bobby won possession in midfield and rolled the ball into my path, a gap opened up so I decided to hit a speculative long-range shot with my right foot. The ball flew in past Gordon Banks of all 'keepers, which stunned not only me, but also the rest of the team. The goal put us 3-1 up, so to let the lead slip was very disappointing even though I was pleased to have scored my first goal for Leeds.

Paul didn't stop there. A few weeks later, he was part of a weakened side that lost to West Brom in a League Cup tie, but he did have the consolation of scoring a 'tap-in' in his side's 4-2 defeat. In the FA Cup, interest ended when Chelsea won a close fourth-round match 1-0, but Leeds' consistency kept them in the race for the Championship. However, four defeats in March dented their challenge. Although they picked up towards the end of the campaign the damage was done and the players had to again settle for the runners-up spot as Liverpool clinched their second title in three years. Nevertheless, their record was exceptional. Leeds had proved their performance the previous season was no fluke; they were now a force to be reckoned with.

The season was particularly memorable because Leeds played in Europe for the first time. Paul made four appearances, the first coming in the team's European bow against the Italian giants Torino.

The atmosphere was very different from a League or domestic cup-tie, and of course we had to adapt, especially away from home, to the different styles of play from our opponents. Torino was a very physical team, and tried to intimidate us with some ferocious tackling. After gaining a slight advantage with a 2-1 win in the opening leg we went to Italy for the return.

Leeds United, 1965/66. From left to right, back row: Bell, Reaney, Lorimer, Belfitt, Cooper. Middle row: Collins (captain), Hunter, Williamson, Sprake, Greenhoff, Madeley. Front row: Johnson, Storrie, Charlton, Peacock, Bremner, Giles, Johanneson.

Paul in the white of Leeds, July 1965.

Leeds' ability was given the sternest test in Torino after skipper Bobby Collins was stretched off after 50 minutes following a horrific challenge by Poletti, the Torino right-back. The result was startling success, but at a cost.

Eric Stanger, *Yorkshire Post*: 'Leeds United fought a magnificent rearguard action at the Stadio Communal, but they paid a heavy price. In adversity they fought every inch of the way and were magnificent. It was one of the greatest victories in Leeds United's history.'

Don Revie commented, 'This was one of the greatest performances I have seen from any team. They proved themselves real professionals. They have given every-thing and have not got an ounce left.'

None of us had ever experienced just how cynical foreign players could be and it was a really tough battle. One horrendous challenge broke Bobby's thigh and ultimately finished his Leeds career. We were determined to progress and did incredibly well to come away with a draw, but the occasion was ruined by Bobby's injury because he was so influential to the side.

Having deputised at left-back in the opening round, Paul played centre-half in a fine 2-1 win against Leipzig, but missed the return leg, which finished 0-0, enabling Leeds to progress. Round three pitched Leeds against Valencia. After a 1-1 draw at Elland Road, Paul took on an anchor midfield role in Spain (although wearing the number 9 shirt). Leeds' 1-0 win, thanks to a Mike O'Grady strike, was a stunning result. The tie would prove to be Paul's last of the campaign, but he would soon be a regular starter.

Richard Ullyatt, *Yorkshire Post*: 'Leeds United proved to the football world that they are never more dangerous than when the odds are piled against them. It was a resounding triumph for this young Leeds team for their tactics, their discipline and their determination to wipe the smear of dirty play from their name. Inexperienced in Europe they may be, but they are learning fast. Madeley has still only a handful of first-team games behind him, but his inexperience never showed. He was the vital midfield link when Leeds attacked and he still managed more than his share of work and of plugging gaps in defence. And it was Madeley who broke up another Valencia

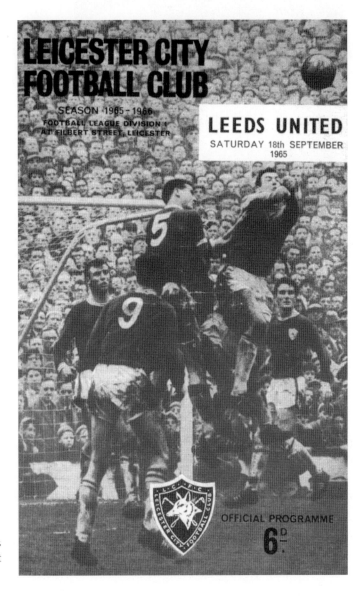

Paul grabbed his first Leeds goal in this League clash at Filbert Street.

attack after 75 minutes to send Mike O'Grady scampering 30 yards for the winner. Valencia went crazy!'

Phil Brown of the *Yorkshire Evening Post* described the youngster's performance: 'Madeley had a grand game and more than maintained the now almost tradition of a United reserve fitting perfectly when called to the first team. Presented as a centre forward, he immediately withdrew deep when play started to a sort of forward centre-half position. He did many useful things indeed in the middle section of the side.'

It was a tremendous performance all-round and it was great to have had a hand in the goal. I looked up and saw Mike about 30 yards away, so I just hoofed it left-footed over their left-back's head and Mike took it from there.

The campaign had gone well and Paul was beginning to receive rave reviews nationally for his versatility.

Sunday Mirror (19 December 1965), Edgar Turner: 'Paul Madeley of Leeds United has his own fan club! And they are pushing the local lad who understudies every position in defence except goal for a new job ... centre forward! Manager Don Revie has a batch of letters, which show just how seriously Paul's sponsor's take the idea, and it might not seem to be a bad one when his all-round ability and size are taken into consideration. Tipping the scales at 12st, six foot, twenty-year-old Madeley has just what it takes to worry defenders. Madeley is one of Elland Road's most valuable assets. Injuries at one time or another have given him the chance to step in and shine at centre-half, wing-half, left-back and right-back. Paul's temporary rating as a reserve does not worry him. The boy from Yorkshire League club Farsley Celtic remains happy and content.'

Leeds had acquitted themselves well in Europe and went on to reach the semi-finals at their first attempt before losing out in a play-off against Real Zaragoza. Not only were the likes of Manchester United, Liverpool and Arsenal taking note, so were the top European sides. Of more significance long-term, Leeds had managed to overcome the loss of Bobby Collins and had a new skipper.

Bobby had been a super player. He could ping the ball with his right foot to anywhere on the park and was incredibly motivational. When Don signed him we had plenty of players, like myself, who could run all day, but you needed someone with an 'old head' to pull the strings and he was the natural player to do that. It was particularly disappointing losing such an influential player as Bobby, however it turned out to be the start of Billy Bremner and Johnny Giles midfield partnership together.

When Billy was made captain I was a bit surprised because to me Big Jack was the natural choice, however Don usually had a long-sighted view and perhaps felt Jack could be a bit headstrong. Billy had an unbelievable never-say-die attitude and was determined to win all the time. Jack on the other hand, needed a big game to stimulate him, and the bigger the game the better he performed. You only have to look at his performances in the 1966 World Cup finals, and many of the massive games we were involved in. You could always rely on Jack in those situations. It was an inspired decision choosing Billy, because it summed up everything we stood for.

Chapter Three

MR VERSATILE

1966/67

During the summer Paul bought his first car, a Vauxhall Viva (registration 644JUB), and like most people in England watched the World Cup on television.

It was a marvellous summer. With everyone in the country caught up in World Cup fever, there was no better time to be a fan or footballer. When we returned for pre-season training there was an incredible buzz around the country with England winning the World Cup and it gave the English lads a reason, not that we needed it, to rib all the Scottish players, which went on forever! Whenever a reference to '66 was available, we took the opportunity!

There was always a big Scottish contingent at the club, so the banter was always there. In training the five-a-side games in particular were extremely hard-fought. We had a mix of teams, and naturally we had many England v Scotland clashes. As time went by, with us all being so competitive, the games were stopped because Don was continually wary about injuries.

The training was tough but there was always time to relax. Being in the midst of the cricket season we'd have an impromptu game, but one annual event all the players looked forward to was a golf tournament organised by Don, with the winner claiming the Don Revie trophy. The competition was incredible, everyone wanted to win, and I got lucky one year. I think that the handicap committee was a little too generous and gave me a few extra shots!

At the start of 1966/67 season Paul found himself in the first team, and celebrated with a goal in a 3-1 win over Manchester United. Tom Holley, *The People*, cited Paul's early goal as a pivotal moment of the match:

A below-strength side whose average age was not much more than 21 gave the vastly more experienced men from Old Trafford a lesson in the use of talent. Every man played his part, and in a magnificent performance showed the more talented (on paper at least) men that skill is not enough and that there is no substitute for skill and hard work. Early on Giles brilliantly exploited Madeley's commanding height by sending the ball high into the middle of the Manchester defence. Madeley, who could consistently out-jump Foulkes, headed Giles's centre home, and from that moment Leeds rarely looked back.

Above: Leeds United, 1966/67. From left to right, back row: Hunter, Peacock, Charlton, Madeley, Gray, Belfitt. Middle row: Revie (manager), Bell, O'Grady, Harvey, Sprake, Johanneson, Johnson, Greenhoff. Front row: Reaney, Collins, Giles, Bremner (captain), Storrie, Lorimer, Cooper.

Left: Alan Peacock, Jack Charlton, Norman Hunter, Paul and Bobby Collins are ready for action.

I scored a few goals as a striker, the best a 'bullet' header against Manchester United, although the 'keeper badly misjudged it!

Leeds' overall form, however, was inconsistent. After being knocked-out of the League Cup following a 7–0 defeat at West Ham, twelve days later a 5–0 defeat at Liverpool was Leeds' fifth in the league.

There were no excuses as we had a full team out on both occasions. West Ham, on their day were pretty useful, especially going forward at home, and it was a big lesson to us. I played left-back and got caught helplessly ball watching for one of the goals. Geoff Hurst scored four that night. He was really on song and still on a high after his hat-trick in the World Cup final against West Germany. It was very rare for us to be beaten by such a heavy score, and it was my heaviest defeat as a player, but sometimes these things happen.

As for the Liverpool clash, it would be remembered as the day Gary threw the ball into his own net! It was very frustrating because on his day Gary could make the most incredible saves, but because we were so much on top in some games he simply lost concentration. Crazy as it may seem I can understand how he made the mistake at Liverpool. He had the ball in his hands when we ran off with our backs to him and was going to throw the ball to Terry

Owzat! Johnny Giles catches his skipper at first slip. Paul and Jimmy Greenhoff are also at close quarters.

Paul (number 9), wheels away to celebrate after a 'bullet' header against Manchester United.

Cooper, but changed his mind mid-throw because he must have thought it would put us under more pressure. In the process disaster struck. It's bizarre and there is no excuse, but it does offer a reason why it happened. I'll never forget the massive roar we heard when he'd thrown the ball into his own goal or the Kop's immediate rendition of 'Careless Hands'!

Fortunately, this was just a temporary loss of form. In the FA Cup, Leeds' run to the semi-finals started with straightforward wins against Crystal Palace 3-0 and West Brom 5-0, though it took three games to get past Sunderland. Following a 1-0 win over Manchester City, Leeds faced Chelsea for a place at Wembley.

The clash against Tommy Docherty's Chelsea side is still one of the most talked about cup matches in the club's history. It was my first major cup semi-final, and I was really looking forward to it. A goal down, we attacked relentlessly and shortly after Terry Cooper had a goal disallowed, Peter appeared to have salvaged a draw when he thumped in a great free kick in the last minute. To everyone's amazement though the referee disallowed the goal, stating that it had been taken too quickly. Losing was bad, but the way we lost was heartbreaking. We were livid, Peter's disallowed goal was a really harsh decision and we felt very bitter in the changing room afterwards. To get knocked out like that was a bitter blow, it was such a big game and we felt particularly aggrieved. It would have been my first FA Cup final so it was a major disappointment.

In Europe, Leeds had embarked on a titanic campaign after overcoming DWS Amsterdam (8-1 on aggregate), a tie in which Paul scored his first European goal in

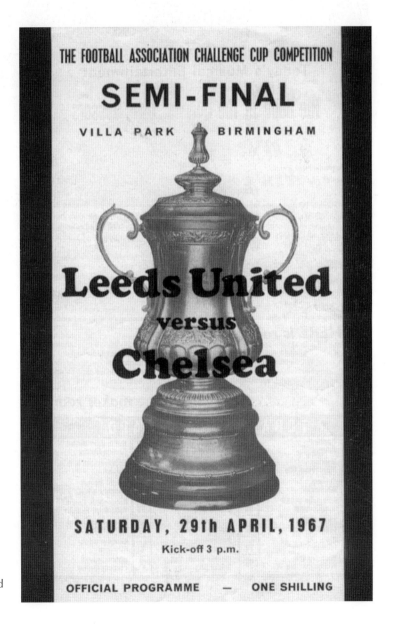

Paul's first FA Cup semi-final when 'Hotshot' Lorimer scored a thunderbolt that was harshly ruled out.

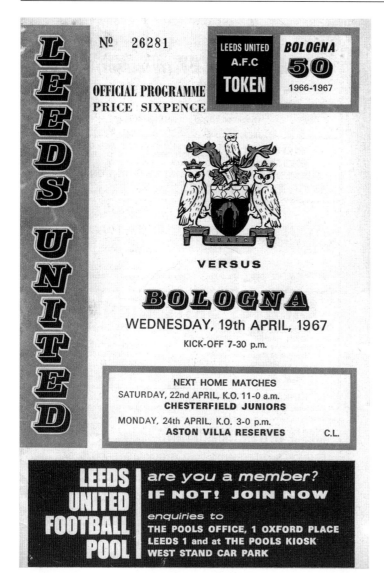

No 26281

LEEDS UNITED A.F.C TOKEN

BOLOGNA 50 1966-1967

OFFICIAL PROGRAMME
PRICE SIXPENCE

VERSUS

BOLOGNA

WEDNESDAY, 19th APRIL, 1967

KICK-OFF 7-30 p.m.

NEXT HOME MATCHES
SATURDAY, 22nd APRIL, K.O. 11-0 a.m.
CHESTERFIELD JUNIORS
MONDAY, 24th APRIL, K.O. 3-0 p.m.
ASTON VILLA RESERVES   C.L.

LEEDS UNITED FOOTBALL POOL | are you a member?
IF NOT! JOIN NOW
enquiries to
THE POOLS OFFICE, 1 OXFORD PLACE
LEEDS 1 and at THE POOLS KIOSK
WEST STAND CAR PARK

Before penalties, drawn ties were settled by tossing of a disc. Billy called correctly!

the home leg, which Leeds won 5-1. The next two rounds would see Leeds face much stiffer opposition … Valencia and Bologna.

We did really well to get through these ties. Valencia were very skilful and held us to a 1-1 draw at Elland Road. In the return though we silenced the crowd when John scored. A Peter Lorimer 'special' sealed a tremendous performance. The Bologna match was incredibly tight and we were a little fortunate to get through after losing the opening leg 1-0. John's penalty in the return levelled matters, but extra time couldn't separate us. Billy won us the tie by winning the toss of a disc. This was the first time I experienced such an event and it was a really surreal atmosphere in the dressing room afterwards.

We shall not be moved! A solid defensive display ensures Leeds' safe passage to a first European final.

In the semi-finals Paul helped Leeds overcome Kilmarnock to reach the club's first European final, where they would face the Yugoslavian giants Dynamo Zagreb.

Unfortunately an injury meant I had to sit out the final, which was really disappointing. The lads battled hard but couldn't break down Dynamo's defence.

In the League, with a return to consistency Leeds finished fourth. On a personal level Paul had broken through. Apart from becoming a regular in the first team, he had remarkably worn every shirt apart from the goalkeeper's and number 11. One of the problems Leeds had experienced was in attack because Alan Peacock was injured and Jim Storrie had moved on. Jimmy Greenhoff was now considered the long-term replacement but he too was injured during the season. Don turned to Paul and amongst a number of outstanding performances was a League clash with Sheffield United at Elland Road during Easter – Leeds won 2-0.

Phil Brown, *Yorkshire Evening Post*: 'The real star was the astonishing Madeley at inside-right for United. As dominant and powerful on the field as he is unobtrusive and quiet off, this young Leeds man stormed through the match with tremendous impact, and his skill on the ball for all his deceptively ungainly look was most striking.

He made Peacock's goal with a glorious wing run and pass back through four or five tackles, and very clearly the determined Blades defence, even using two centre-halves in Mallender and Matthewson, did not know how to stop him. Beautifully as Giles again played, Madeley was man of the match, and when you remember his defensive strength when required it makes his development highly interesting indeed. Just now as a forward he cannot be dropped.'

John Helm, *Yorkshire News*: 'The rise of Paul Madeley is another pleasing aspect of the curriculum. As a footballer he rose in stature no small measure, and in the home game against Sheffield gave a sparkling display; probably his best yet. He made one goal with superb ease and skill, beating three men to do it, and his versatility seems boundless. Madeley has now played in many positions for Leeds and would no doubt pull on the 'keeper's jersey with distinction if asked.'

With Paul's elevation into the first team, the future beckoned for one of the country's most-talented young stars. During the summer, Paul was chosen as part of a powerful FA XI that won the Expo 1967 tournament in Montreal. Playing in all three games, he completed the half-back line alongside his Leeds team-mate Norman Hunter and Brian Labone of Everton.

It had been some season for the twenty-two year old, who in numerous articles was dubbed 'Mr Versatile'. Don Revie was continually asked how he would best use his utility player. In an interview conducted by Bill Mallinson, *Daily Mail*, the Leeds manager would not be pinned down.

He is the most valuable player that a club can have. You never know he is about. He is so quiet, trains hard and has never grumbled about being moved so many times. I may have problems if he had a settled position. Suppose he was injured and I had to find somebody to fill his place! He is unique. I have never known another player like him all the time I have been in football. I can't give this lad enough praise for what he has done for Leeds United. But as to what happens in the future we will have to wait and see.

Regarding an England call-up and what jersey would suit him best, Revie reeled off to Mallinson: 'Right-half, centre-half, right-back, left-back or left-half... and if they were short in the forward line they could use him there too!'

Defensively, I was comfortable on either flank, although the left side was a bit more awkward, because I was naturally right-footed. It wasn't an ideal situation as a full-back, but I never really found it harder to defend on one side or another. As for midfield, I'd fill the defensive midfield role in front of the back four, or in certain games take on a man-marking job. Playing in attack was a surprise to me because we had Rod Belfitt, and most of my early games had been in defence.

I partnered, at different times, Peter, Eddie and Jimmy. I also partnered Alan Peacock; some people thought we had a similar look of each other and dubbed us the 'twin' strikers. Although he had suffered with knee injuries, he was still a class act, but was past his peak. I was no more than a stopgap though. Fortunately, my pace gave defenders problems and I was a fair header of the ball, but I was not a striker. Of all the positions I played it was my least favourite, however when Don asked me to play in attack I did my best. Although I was happy to play in attack, it was not my preferred choice.

When I faced the likes of Bobby Moore, Ron Harris or Tommy Smith I did feel in awe, however when I came up against George Best, Denis Law, Bobby Charlton and Jimmy Greaves, although I didn't always feel on a par ability-wise, I knew my defensive skills would stand me in good stead.

I wasn't the only player to switch position, because Don converted Terry Cooper from a left-winger to left-back with devastating effect. Initially he broke into the side as a left-wing

Footballer by day
... businessman in
the afternoon.

replacement for Albert Johanneson. Albert on his day was superb, but he wasn't as tough as Terry, especially in away matches when we had to dig in and battle. Switching Terry was a masterstroke. He had played the odd game at left-back, but replaced Willie Bell on a regular basis. Terry's anticipation was brilliant, and often he outthought opponents. When he went on the overlap opposing full-backs soon discovered that he could tackle harder than they could!

I was delighted how the season had gone. The atmosphere at the club was great, the squad was coming together and we feared nobody. We couldn't wait for matches. In training we worked hard in the early part of the week and eased down towards the back end, because Don was always on tenterhooks that one of us might get injured. He'd say that's enough lads, and he never really changed. The five-a-sides were always challenging and the coaches changed routines to keep us on our toes. As a player I'd achieved my initial objective of securing a first-team place, more important I knew I was at the right club at the right time. Everyone in the game knew it, we had a young side and our best years were in front of us. I now wanted to win major honours, especially a League title and the FA Cup. I knew it would only be a matter of time.

It was also an exciting time at home. My brothers had started a business and from the early stages of my football career John used to tell me that I had to get into the first team more often because we needed the publicity!

Chapter Four

UP FOR THE CUP

1967/68

Though Leeds had become established in the upper echelons of the game, having still to win major honours was the aim. Asked by journalists whether after four years chasing promotion and titles some of his players were burned out, Don Revie replied: 'I don't think so, we are still a young side and I am looking for them to have matured and to play even better this season. Much rests on the characters of the players themselves. I think they have there hearts set, like all others at Leeds, on winning something as a reward for our disappointments and setbacks in the last three years.'

Despite the sentiments, Revie's team began their league campaign poorly, winning just one game in their opening five league matches. With Peacock coming to the end of his career (he would leave in October 1967), and just four goals being scored, Revie entered the transfer market and splashed out a club record £100,000 on Sheffield United's star centre forward Mick Jones.

Results soon picked up, the highlight being a 7-0 win against Chelsea, avenging their FA Cup semi-final defeat. The addition of Jones gave the team a focal point in attack, by Christmas they were back in the title hunt. A 2-1 win against Wolves on December 23 was the first of six consecutive wins. At the turn of the year, media reports suggested that Paul Madeley was the subject of a £100,000 bid from Arsenal as a replacement for their Scottish international Ian Ure, who was for sale at £125,000.

Speaking to Bill Mallinson *Daily Mail*, Don Revie was adamant that Madeley was going nowhere because Paul was 'worth his weight in gold'. As for twenty-three-year-old Madeley who had played 96 games for Leeds, 16 being in Europe, he was happy at Leeds despite not having a regular position in the side.

I was extremely flattered, but regarding a move to London, I didn't have any hankering for the bright lights.

The run continued into April, as the team remained unbeaten for fourteen matches. In early January, without Charlton, Bremner and Gray, Leeds demolished Southampton 5-0, with Paul (playing at centre-half) scoring twice from corner kicks. The goals were his first of the season, and would be the only brace of his career.

Paul Madeley, the deputy centre-half who became a scoring sensation, blasts the first of his TWO goals past 'keeper Eric Martin . . .   It's Madeley again, stabbing out his left foot to squeeze the ball inside an upright.

Mine's a double! Paul scores twice against Southampton in a 5-0 win.

The *Yorkshire Post* was impressed with both Leeds and their auxiliary centre-half:

Leeds once again risk finishing the season feeling like the greedy child with too many sweets in its fist to get its hand out of the jar, unable to let one or two go to keep the others. They are already in the last four of the League Cup and in the last eight of the Fairs Cup and are joint second favourites for the FA Cup. Their lofty place in the First Division was not the most important achievement won in this match, nor was it the absence of any sign of strain in a team who have an average of two games a week this season. For me here was the final proof that any who may doubt it that Leeds have found and filled modern football's surest prescription for success; a squad capable of withstanding injury blows to any department, who do not need reserves because there are 17 first-team players. If any club in the land are capable of clearing all that is on their plate without suffering the heartburn of total failure Leeds are that club.

Madeley is generally rated the best all-rounder in the League. Here he also looked the best centre-half, bringing to the game all the quiet, almost detached authority he wears off the field. He did not appear to be exceptionally fast yet he once again matched one of football's 'fliers' stride for stride, and I would back him to pull away from almost anyone else Southampton had. With his deceptive, shuffling style he did not seem sharp enough to create any special menace in penalty-area raids and yet superb positional sense won him two goals.

Full of confidence Leeds faced Derby County in a League Cup semi-final clash. To date they had disposed of Luton Town 3-1, Bury 3-0, Sunderland 2-0 and Stoke City 2-0 before their clash with the Rams, managed by Brian Clough, a young manager making his name in the game and not afraid to speak his mind. The run had summed

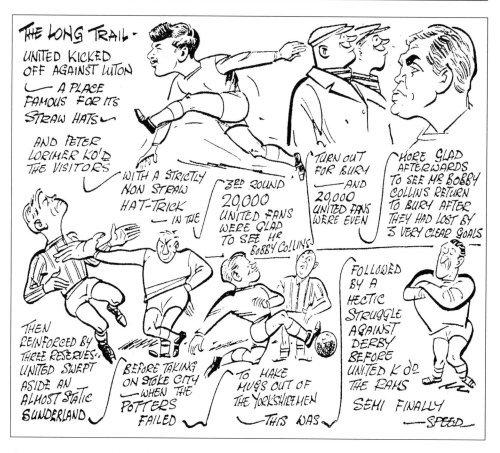

Cartoon capers as Leeds reach Wembley.

up Madeley's versatility and value to Leeds. After missing the Luton tie through injury, he filled in for Terry Cooper at left-back against Bury, before replacing Jack Charlton in the win at Sunderland. Injury saw him sit out the Stoke clash, but he was back against Derby for the semi-final first leg at centre forward with Mick Jones cup-tied and Jones' replacement Rod Belfitt injured.

On the eve of the match, Paul was interviewed by Frank Clough, *The Sun*. In 'Mr Versatile', Paul gave his reaction to two £100,000 bids linking him with London clubs.

Plain barmy! Prices like these are ridiculous, out of all proportion. I think the only players worth that sort of money are the specialist, the blokes who regularly score goals, and that's not me. Mind you, I admit I am dead chuffed when I read it. It does my confidence all the world of good. It is flattering but it doesn't worry me. I don't want to leave United because I believe that in a couple of years it is going to be a fantastic team and I would love to be a part of it. If the club said I could go if I wanted, well I would think about it and take the best financial offer I suppose, but I don't want that to happen. I have lived in Leeds all my life; my family and friends are all here and so is my wallpaper business, which is coming along quite nicely.

Anyway, the boss keeps telling us we are the best team in the world. I would be a fool to leave that sort of team, wouldn't I?

As for playing in nine positions, I wore nine different shirts, that's all. There are only three positions the way football is played today – defenders, schemers and attackers. I look on myself as a defender; I joined Leeds as a centre-half, though I have tried the others as well when they have needed me. It doesn't bother me where I play. United pay my wages so if they want me to play in goal, I go in goal. When you are young and just hoping to get a crack at the first team, you have got to take your chance when it comes, wherever you are told to play.

Derby may have been in Division Two, but it was a really tight game, which ended in a 1-1 draw. Leeds were more than satisfied to have home advantage to come in the return.

With Big Jack out I reverted to centre-half. It was another tight encounter but we came through 3-2 to win 4-3 on aggregate, setting up a Wembley date with Arsenal. Rod Belfitt

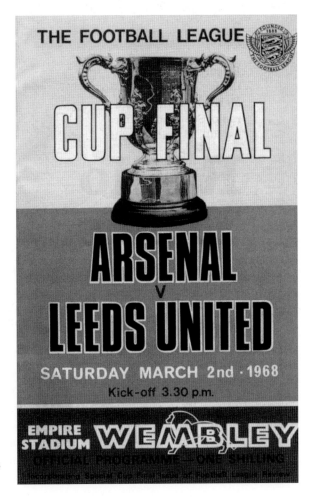

Not a classic … nonetheless
a historic day

had a great game, scoring twice. It was a very happy dressing room after, because for a number of us it would be our first Wembley cup final

During the build-up to the final, Paul won the *London Evening Standard* Footballer of the Month award. In an article 'The Priceless Reserve' printed on the day of final, Don Revie spelled out what Madeley brought to Leeds United.

Madeley's qualities are priceless because they are the very foundation of success in modern football; they give continuity and teamwork at a time when talent is in short supply, fat signing-on fees are paid on transfer and players demand a move once they lose their place. Versatile players are essential when tactics change from week to week, according to the opposition or the nature of the fixture, and sides are chosen from a compact first-team squad. Money cannot buy him! He is a great club-man, very fit, dedicated and contented, and we cannot afford to let a player like that go.

In the article, Paul was laid back about his best position:

I am very happy at getting a place where I fit in. My preference is to be a defender rather than an attacker. I used to want to be a back because of the chance to strike at goal in an overlap, but now centre-half or defensive wing-half would be my choice because I think they are the easiest to play. It's inferred that I don't command a regular place, but I get in as many games as first-team players. Besides being in the senior squad of a top club like Leeds keeps you in the hunt for honours and brings you matches like today at Wembley. I might lose that chance if I moved elsewhere.

Revie had a dilemma for the final with everyone reporting fit. In the end, Madeley was handed the number 9 shirt, Rod Belfitt having to be satisfied with a place on the bench.

Arsenal v. Leeds United, League Cup final

ARSENAL: Furnell, Storey, McNab, McLintock, Simpson, Ure, Radford, Jenkins (Neill), Graham, Sammels, Armstrong

LEEDS UNITED: Sprake, Reaney, Cooper, Bremner, Charlton, Hunter, Lorimer, Greenhoff, Lorimer, Madeley, Giles, Gray (Belfitt)

Even though we were involved in other competitions the build up to the League Cup final was very exciting. It was my first major domestic final and the anticipation throughout the club was enormous. Everyone was so determined to win after losing to Liverpool a few years earlier. Rod was a shade unlucky to miss out because he'd only missed one match of the run, but I was delighted to be playing. For every player, to play at Wembley was a big ambition. I couldn't wait to experience the occasion, and of course our fans like ourselves desperately wanted to win a major trophy.

Paul in action during his first Wembley final. Here he challenges George Graham and John Radford.

Arriving at the stadium and seeing all the fans congregating on the approach to the Twin Towers was brilliant. Walking around the pitch beforehand, the atmosphere was fantastic. You could sense the occasion and anticipation, even though the League Cup had only been going a few years and didn't have the FA Cup's history. Waiting in the tunnel and walking out, though nerve-wracking, was a wonderful experience. The noise when you emerged may have been deafening but it gave you a real adrenaline rush. It was very different to other stadiums and very special.

The match turned out to be a poor game, but Terry Cooper's 'controversial' first-half strike proved sufficient to beat Arsenal and finally remove the 'bridesmaid' label from Revie's team. Journalists, though not impressed, realised the significance of the result.

Frank McGhee, *Daily Mirror*: 'The most jaw-aching yawn ever seen at Wembley, but Leeds were worth their win and their trophy. They produced the better players and played the better football.'

Ronald Crowther, *Daily Mail*: 'Manager Don Revie offered no excuses, he had no reason to do so. For this was the cold and clinical approach to cup winning, and such rigid restraint rarely gives rise to spectacle. Regarding Leeds goal that Arsenal debated vociferously, it was a chance superbly accepted ... Cooper's calmness proved decisive.'

It's there! Terry Cooper (hidden behind Jack Charlton, No.5) grabs the winner.

Eric Stanger, *Yorkshire Post:*

> Leeds, four times foiled of a rich prize in the last four seasons, played this game as they would a cup-tie in Europe ... tight, taking no risks and leaving no loophole behind on the occasions they did move upfield. It does not make for bright entertainment but it is the result, which is remembered long after the details of the play are forgotten. United got the result they wanted by giving nothing away and by strict application of every man to his task and attention to detail.
>
> Arsenal tackled hard, often more sharply than Leeds, but like so many teams before them they found movements they had begun so well in midfield destroyed by the power of the Leeds defence as they approached the penalty area. Bremner led his men with such courage and determination that in the last 20 minutes when Leeds were battling away for dear life as Arsenal strove desperately to snatch an equaliser, he was prepared to take on the whole Arsenal side if necessary. One hand was already on the Cup and while Bremner had breath no one was going to wrest it from him. Now Leeds have gained their first honour, perhaps they will be all the better for having got it out of their system that they were always fated to finish runners–up.

The Leeds camp was ecstatic:

Don Revie: 'I don't think we have seen the best of this team. No matter what I said to them before we played Arsenal, it could not quite remove the nagging

The *Yorkshire Evening Post Sports Echo* edition reports from Wembley.

question: "Are we going to miss it again?" But they have answered that for themselves. This win makes up for all those other disappointments and it will help us tremendously from now on and will give the players confidence and make them believe in themselves as winners.'

Billy Bremner: 'It was not a great spectacle but I'd rather play like that and win, than play well and lose. It is a great load of our minds.'

Jack Charlton: 'We came to win and not put on a showpiece. We will take some whacking now that we have got one under our belts. Now we know we can win trophies.'

As for the goalscorer Terry Cooper, the twenty-three-year-old left-back told reporters he'd dreamt all week about scoring on his Wembley debut. 'It was the same dream every night until Friday. I was dribbling with the ball and kept falling over both the ball and my own feet. Then 60 yards out I gave it a crack. In the dream the ball landed in the back of the net. Then on Friday I dreamed that I shot the ball into the net without falling over the ball or anything. Footballers are always dreaming about scoring, but it has never happened to me before. As for the goal, I thought I had lifted it too much, but it was just right.'

Celebration time. Jimmy Greenhoff, Paul and Johnny Giles are delighted with their first 'major' honour.

The players celebrate their League Cup victory.

It was always going to be tight game so we knew the first goal could prove crucial. I remember our goal more than anything. The game had no real pattern when we won a corner. At the time we employed a tactic at corners where Jack stood in front of their goalkeeper, which made it awkward when coming out for crosses. Big Jack was terrific in the air and very intimidating, the tactic brought him a stack of goals. Eddie swung over a great cross, Jack as usual was standing near the goalkeeper, I put in a great leap without getting anywhere near the ball, and between us we stopped him getting near it. The ball fell to Terry who lashed it home. The biggest trouble we had was trying to catch him after he'd scored when he ran off to celebrate!

The Arsenal players were furious because they felt Jack and myself had impeded their 'keeper Jim Furnell. It wasn't a blatant foul, but fortunately the referee saw nothing wrong. However, we weren't the only team to make challenges like that, it was part of the game in that era. There have been a number of pictures where Big Jack is in the vicinity and you can see me running in and jumping to try and head the ball before the ball dropped for Terry to fire home. The referee was close by and had a good view, so I'm not sure what all the fuss was about.

This was my first match at Wembley, and the pitch didn't suit my style. Apart from being energy sapping, I was skidding a lot and the lush turf meant the ball didn't bounce truly. Overall I had a poor match until Rod came on for Eddie. I switched to midfield to help protect the lead and played a lot better than I had been doing up front. I was delighted to get away from the striking role.

It was certainly no classic, but it was an important victory at the time. It was a fairly bad-tempered game and a tough test, but the result gave us a lot of confidence. We'd been runners-up so many times; it was a great feeling to finally win a major honour. We all realised how important it was that we won because it was a breakthrough for us. Going up for the cup and the lap of honour were everything I imagined; the overall feeling in the dressing room afterwards though was a mixture of elation and relief. The celebrations went on with a civic reception where thousands of fans welcomed us home, it was brilliant.

On 20 March 1968 Paul became the first Leeds United player to wear all ten outfield shirts, following a League clash against Chelsea when he wore the number 11 shirt. Leeds' 0-0 draw kept their title aspirations going whilst at the same time they marched on in the FA Cup, following victories over Derby County, Nottingham Forest, and Bristol City to book a quarter-final spot. The performances were professional rather than spectacular, with the Forest and Bristol clashes being best remembered for the performances of Leeds' deputy goalkeepers!

Against Forest, Gary had to go off briefly; I was delighted to see Norman go in goal because I didn't fancy it. They managed to grab one goal before Gary's return but we eventually won 2-1. Against Bristol, we were ahead 2-0 when Gary got himself sent off after a clash with Chris Garland. This time Peter went in, and managed to keep a clean sheet.

In the last eight, Leeds faced Sheffield United at Elland Road...

In this newspaper shot, Paul settles a tight FA Cup quarter-final clash with Sheffield United.

A blunder from Gary Sprake costs Leeds a return trip to Wembley.

I played number 8 and Don always made a point about following shots in, which I did on this occasion. Their 'keeper parried a shot and I just managed to poke the ball in from a tight angle to nick us a 1-0 win. After the game I was asked to give a post-match radio interview for the first time. I told the reporter that I was surprised when the ball came my way. It wasn't exactly the most riveting of interviews!

We played Sheffield again a week later in the League. I grabbed one of our goals in a comfortable 3-0 win before incredibly scoring at Spurs in the next match, a game we won 2-1. This was the first time I'd scored in three consecutive games for Leeds; Norman gave me some stick. Suddenly I was known as 'goal-a-game' Madeley!

Leeds drew Everton in the semi-finals as the team stayed in contention for the title, although they suffered a setback with a 3-2 loss at Stoke City a few days before the cup clash at Old Trafford. The players had a chance to create a piece of history if they won because they would become the first team to reach both domestic cup finals at Wembley in the same season.

Paul grabs a goal against West Brom in a League clash at Elland Road.

Arsenal's Bobby Gould and Paul lunge for a cross – unfortunately for the Leeds man, the ball deflects off his shoulder past his own 'keeper.

Having already won one cup, we were determined to double-up, but it wasn't to be. Gary made a mess of a clearance, and they scored from the resultant penalty after Jack had handled their goal bound shot on the line. Sadly it would not be his last big-match blunder. It was a huge disappointment losing a second successive FA Cup semi-final.

Despite the setback Leeds had a lot to play for, both at home and in Europe, but the games were coming thick and fast. Following a 3-1 win over West Brom the title race was wide open with Leeds challenging Manchester City, Manchester United and Liverpool. With three matches to go Leeds faced Bill Shankly's side at Elland Road on 4 May. Don Revie's described the match as 'the most important in the club's history'. After taking the lead, two quick-fire goals gave Liverpool victory.

Leeds' challenge was effectively over. Tom Holley of the *Yorkshire Post* concluded that in the club's 63rd game of the season, 'absolute fatigue, both mentally and physically' had thwarted Leeds title bid, in what had been a hectic season. A 4-3 defeat at Arsenal resulted in Revie resting eight of his first team (not Paul) for the final League game of the season at Burnley. A third consecutive defeat meant a fourth place finish for the second successive year, but there was still one game left as Leeds chased European glory.

Flight to the battlefields of Europe.

The team had enjoyed the challenge of their third European campaign, and after reaching a semi-final and final previously were determined to go all the way this time. Leeds' campaign began against Spora Luxembourg, winning 16-0 on aggregate, a club record; Paul scored in the 9-0 win at Elland Road.

Phil Brown, *Yorkshire Evening Post*: 'The bigger they are the harder they fall, but the bigger they are the harder they knock you down.'

When Leeds won the opening leg of their clash with Partizan Belgrade 2-1 in the next round, it seemed their passage was all but assured. That they struggled to a 1-1 draw for a 3-2 aggregate victory puzzled many, but they were through to a third round clash with Hibernian. Prior to the opening leg, Paul was involved in a club *v.* country debate after Don Revie withdrew him from winning his first Under-23 cap for England after being selected at centre-half to face Italy at Nottingham. With Leeds having an important Fairs Cup match scheduled for the same night, Revie pulled his player out of the clash.

Revie told reporters: 'I wouldn't have taken this step and contacted Sir Alf Ramsey if it hadn't been absolutely essential. He granted Paul's release without hesitation and we're very grateful for that. It's a bit hard on the players when this sort of thing

Paul leads the charge against Rangers during a frantic Fairs Cup clash.

happens. I hate having to do it but after all we pay their wages all the year and I think they understand the position. I've apologised to Paul, but I'm certain he'll get another chance the way he's playing.'

The first leg was a drab affair. Leeds' 1-0 win meant a tough return and they were made to work extremely hard to claim a draw on a bone-hard pitch. The *Yorkshire Evening Post* reporter Phil Brown said that Leeds had advanced 2-1 on aggregate by 'sheer guts, courage and unstinted effort'.

Leeds travelled back to Scotland for their quarter-final tie where they faced 80,000 hostile Rangers supporters. Following a 0-0 draw reporters believed that the result ranked as high as anything United had achieved under Revie.

Phil Brown' *Yorkshire Evening Post*: 'United struck one of the heaviest blows that Scotland's soccer pride has had to take for many a year at Ibrox. They had already played a long season, but they sailed through the game as if it was in September.'

As for the return at Elland Road, the match was described as 'a moment of truth', and Leeds came through with flying colours.

Phil Brown' *Yorkshire Evening Post*: 'Rangers played well and played hard, but United's response was splendid after having to sweat to hold the incisive start the

Almost there! An 'away goal' by Leeds' auxiliary centre forward proved crucial in this clash.

Scots made. As at Ibrox, United got hold of the game, and then dictated its course largely.'

We had some close battles, especially against Rangers. I remember the first leg in particular because we played extremely well in terms of the physical aspect of the game. Naturally they had a partisan crowd, but we coped pretty easily, we weren't under too much pressure. I missed the second leg, but a 2-0 win set up our third cup semi-final of the season, this time against our third Scottish opponents ... Dundee.

In the opening leg at Dens Park we gained an advantage after drawing 1-1. With Mick injured, Don played me in attack and I managed to grab our goal, which was very pleasing, but more important, we had an away goal.

Paul Madeley's goal was his second in the campaign and tenth of the season. The total would be his best ever for a campaign. Having played in attack for the opening leg, he was back in defence for the return following an injury to Jack Charlton. In a lethargic display, Leeds squeezed through to their second European final.

Phil Brown, *Yorkshire Evening Post*: 'Leeds were completely played out mentally and physically by their mammoth programme ... To force any more competitive games on them would be football cruelty to a side that a few weeks back could have taken on any team in Europe.'

The pitch was rock hard, but Eddie's goal gave us a 2-1 aggregate win to set up a final clash against the Hungarian giants Ferencvaros. The final was held back until the start of the next season, which I was not too upset about because it had been a really tough campaign. It had gone really well and I couldn't wait for the new season because we really felt we had a chance to go for the Championship. The team had a good balance and more importantly we'd won a major trophy.

Chapter Five

CHAMPIONS!

1968/69

Confidence was high as Leeds United embarked on the new season. First, however, there was unfinished business in the Fairs Cup.

Leeds United v. Ferencvaros, Fairs Cup final first leg

LEEDS UNITED: Sprake, Reaney, Cooper, Bremner (captain), Charlton, Hunter, Lorimer, Madeley, Jones (Belfitt), Giles (Greenhoff), Gray

FERENCVAROS: Geczi, Novak, Pancsics, Havasi, Szucs, Juhasz, Szoke, Varga, Albert, Rakosi, Fenyvesi (Balint)

Due to the match occurring in the middle of a local bank holiday and coverage live on television (rare in the 1960s), the game only attracted just over 25,000 fans. Ferencavros packed their defence and relied on the counter-attack.

I played alongside Mick Jones in attack. It was a real struggle because they stuck nine men behind the ball. In the end, we were delighted Mick grabbed us a first-leg lead. It gave us a slender advantage and something to defend in the second leg.

As in the League Cup final the only goal of the match was controversial. Lorimer floated a corner under the Ferencvaros bar; Geczi, put off by Charlton, missed the ball completely. Charlton touched the ball on for Jones to scramble it over the line. Leeds tried for a second, but in the end was indebted to Sprake who saved brilliantly from Rakosi.

Fans and pundits wondered whether a one-goal cushion would be sufficient. Phil Brown of the *Yorkshire Evening Post* was concerned, but had not lost hope. 'That old enemy of Leeds United's faulty finishing leaves them with a hard row to hoe ... but so often they have found their best form when facing high odds ... that all may be well.'

Speaking afterwards to the *Yorkshire Post,* Don Revie was unhappy with Ferencvaros' tactics. 'They were body checking, deliberately handling and obstructing ... Some of it was diabolically clever and screened ... It will be tough now in Budapest but we have faced tough ones before. We would have liked a two-goal lead but keeping a clean sheet was an achievement.'

Up for the Fairs Cup!

Leeds turned their attention to their Division One campaign and began in terrific style, winning their opening four fixtures. Paul played in the opening clash at Southampton, but picked up an injury that would keep him out for a month. At one stage it seemed he might miss the second leg of the Fairs Cup final, along with John Giles who was also injured. Unlike the Irishman though, Paul proved his fitness four days before the final in a 2-1 win against Wolves. The team's victory was their sixth from their opening seven League games. Once again they were among the pacesetters.

Phil Brown commented in the *Yorkshire Evening Post* that Madeley provided the 'brightest note' in United. Brown added: 'Madeley had a beautifully balanced and judged game in both attack and defence, closing that central gap, going up into attack and helping Charlton to combat the wiles, some 'villainous', of Dougan.'

The players flew to Budapest determined to triumph, but knew they would face their most severe test yet in Europe. In front of a hostile capacity crowd of 76,000 the players realised that Ferencvaros would be a totally different proposition to the side that they faced at Elland Road ... they were right.

Right: Advantage Leeds ... following the first leg.

Below: Paul and Norman Hunter fail to stop Ferencvaros forward Szoke, but the 'keeper saves the day.

Ferencvaros v. Leeds United, Fairs Cup final second leg:

FERENCVAROS: Geczi, Novak, Pancsics, Havasi, Szucs, Juhasz, Szoke (Kraba), Varga, Albert, Rakosi, Katona

LEEDS UNITED: Sprake, Reaney, Cooper, Bremner (captain), Charlton, Hunter, O'Grady, Lorimer, Jones, Madeley, Hibbitt (Bates)

With Giles sidelined, Paul filled his midfield berth alongside Bremner and Hibbitt. The return was an enthralling encounter as Leeds absorbed wave upon wave of Ferencvaros attacks. The Leeds defence was resolute though and held out for a magnificent win. Hero on the night was Gary Sprake, who had his finest game in a Leeds shirt.

The second leg was a hard-fought rear-guard action, and we were indebted to Gary who made a number of world-class saves. He was sensational and his performance won us the cup. They had some cracking players, so to hold them was a great achievement. The celebrations in the dressing room and all the way home were fantastic; it was one flight that went extremely quickly! At the civic reception again thousands of fans greeted us: it was a wonderful night. The win gave us a lot of confidence for the League campaign because suddenly we'd won two trophies in a few months. We feared nobody and knew that we could give anyone a game.

This was no match for the faint-hearted.

After the match Revie was a relieved manager: 'When we got into those final few minutes my heart nearly stopped beating. As the final whistle drew nearer every minute seemed like an hour.'

The media were unanimous in their praise of the team's achievement:

Alan Thompson, *Daily Express*: 'Fingernails may need a manicure, all adrenaline has been drained and the heart has taken a hammering, but Leeds, those masters of deep and discipline defence, held out against an onslaught of green-shirted Hungarians that lasted for almost the entirety of this game. How they did it is something of a miracle.'

Frank McGhee, *The Mirror*: 'Leeds at last have fought their way into British football's hall of fame – they can now point to a trophy every club in Europe would be proud to possess.'

R.H. Williams, *Daily Telegraph*: 'If 0-0 suggests a boring war of attrition it could not be more misleading ... Leeds were engaged in the battle of their lives against a fast, fluent and clever Hungarian side who would probably have humbled any other defence in the world.'

Phil Brown, *Yorkshire Evening Post:* 'One of the most exciting goal-less draws ever played. Their defence, famous as it has become, had its finest-ever game. They were always there when it came to the key moment, when the shots or header was to be taken. Nobody shirked a thing, even when lungs and legs were straining against the onslaught. If a man beat them they turned around and chased him. Their fitness

The magnificent eleven ... From left to right, back row: Hunter, Bates, Madeley, Sprake, Charlton, O'Grady. Front row: Cooper, Bremner, Reaney, Jones, Lorimer.

Celebration time … with Coca-Cola!

The boys are back in town … with the Fairs Cup.

Leeds United, 1968/69. From left to right, back row: Reaney, Charlton, Madeley, Jones, Harvey, Sprake, Belfitt, Gray, Hunter. Front row: Hibbitt, Giles, Cooper, Bremner (captain), O'Grady, Bates, Lorimer, Johanneson.

furthermore, matched their determination. Don Revie deserves his own tribute for the way he has steered the side to a couple of coveted trophies against massive opposition.'

Returning triumphantly, Leeds ran out at Leicester City, but looked clearly jaded and could only manage a 1-1 draw thanks to Madeley's first goal of the campaign. For someone not renowned for his goal-scoring, this was his third in four seasons at Filbert Street!

Leicester's ground was certainly becoming a lucky one for me. It was bizarre, but I wasn't complaining.

A week later Leeds faced league-leaders Arsenal. In a thrilling match Leeds won 2-0. Tom Holley of the *Yorkshire Post* felt that Don Revie's team was genuine title contenders. 'There is still a long way to go, but on this form I cannot see anyone to beat them...Leeds were tighter in defence, superior in midfield and more penetrative in attack.'

Undefeated, Leeds travelled to Maine Road to play the defending champions but slipped to a 3-1 defeat. Disappointed, the players bounced back with three wins, before a crushing 5-1 defeat at Burnley.

The match at Turf Moor was a big turning point of the season, because we tightened up defensively and began to grind out results.

After three 0-0 draws, another Madeley goal settled a tight game at Coventry City, which began a run that would yield 13 wins in 16 games as Leeds' title challenge gathered pace. With Giles back in the side, Paul switched between attack, alongside Jones, and left-back, with Cooper struggling with an injury. There were some exceptional results; the pick being three consecutive League wins at the turn of the year against Burnley 6-1, Newcastle United 2-1 and Manchester United 2-1.

Tom Holley of the *Yorkshire Post* was full of praise following the demolition of Burnley. 'After this magnificent display who can doubt that Leeds are still capable of brilliant attacking football? In a terrific first-half 'blitz', they took Burnley by the scruff of the neck to hand out a real spanking.'

We were playing with a lot of confidence and expected to get a result in every game. The Burnley result was a bit special. My goal at Newcastle on Boxing Day was a long-range effort, which I was quite pleased with. I told the lads after it was a belated Christmas present to them! The Christmas games always came thick and fast, so we were confined to barracks, but it was a job that had to be done and a small price to pay for being a footballer. We always had a club party where the kids came along; it was always terrific fun.

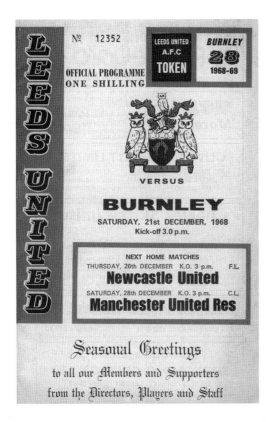

The turning point of the season as Leeds hammer Burnley.

The only disappointment for Leeds had been a defeat in an FA Cup third round replay by Sheffield Wednesday, after Paul had seen a goal harshly disallowed in the opening clash at Hillsborough with the score level at 1-1. Initially the goal had been awarded before the referee Mr Jim Finney penalised Charlton for an infringement.

Leeds may have been out of both domestic cups (Paul grabbed Leeds' goal in a 2-1 fourth round defeat at Crystal Palace), but their defence of the Fairs Cup was going well. The campaign had begun against Standard Liege, where having drawn 0-0 in Belgium, Leeds found themselves 2-0 behind in the return. Pulling on all their reserves, they came back with three goals in the last 20 minutes for a famous 3-2 win. The next round saw another remarkable win, when after losing 2-0 in the first leg Napoli levelled the tie 2-2 in the return. As against Bologna in 1966/67, the match would be decided on the toss of a disc, and once again Bremner broke Italian hearts by choosing correctly.

We couldn't believe it, but those were the rules. Eventually UEFA brought in the penalty shoot out, which whilst not perfect can be very exciting, as is the 'golden goal'.

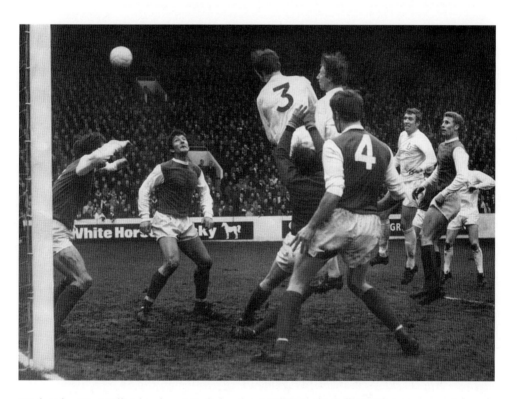

Wednesday Woe! Officials rule out Paul's header at Hillsborough in the FA Cup.

Sprake gathers cleanly to deny Siemensmeyer of Hanover. Paul and Jack Charlton look on.

The German side Hannover 96 were Leeds' next opponents, but the tie was all but over after their visit to Elland Road just before Christmas following a 5-1 defeat. The return would not take place until February.

Wins over QPR and Coventry City kept the pressure on the league leaders, but the win against the Sky Blues came at a cost, as an injury sidelined Paul for a month, limiting Revie'e tactical options. In his absence a 2-0 win against Ipswich Town finally overhauled Liverpool at the top of the table, and for the first time since the early stages of the season both teams had played the same number of games. With 13 matches left Revie's team was in pole position to clinch their first Division One title.

Leeds duly completed a 7-2 aggregate win against Hannover 96, and after a month on the sidelines Paul returned for Leeds' fourth-round clash against Ujpesti Dozsa. Unfortunately, it would not be a happy return as the Hungarians recorded a 1-0 win. However, the team bounced back immediately with a crushing 5-1 win against Stoke City. Only nine League games remained. Leeds looked unstoppable, and only had one challenger ... Liverpool.

According to national papers the title race was over.

Follow that!' headlined one tabloid. ' "We are the Champions!" roared the army of day-trippers from Elland Road before the game started. Ninety minutes, five goals, and two points later, even that hard-to-convince gentlemen Bill Shankly would have been struggling to put together any kind of case for his beloved Liverpool.'

After the game, Stoke manager Tony Waddington commented. 'They murdered us. There isn't a better-equipped side in the country. If they have weaknesses, they are so well disguised you can't find them. When people say they are a dull side without flair, I feel amused. It is inconceivable to imagine them failing this time.'

Prior to a 0-0 draw with Wolves, Leeds' defence of the Fairs Cup ended following a 2-0 defeat in Hungary.

We weren't that upset. Our main objective was the League, so we could now concentrate on the remaining games. I picked up a knock at Wolves so missed a couple of games, but I was back for the run-in.

Following a hard-fought draw at West Brom, Leeds defeated Arsenal 2-1 and Leicester City 2-0. Revie described the win at Highbury as arguably his team's 'best of the season'. Leeds were the only side to record a 'double' over the Gunners and the result, according to Revie, was a 'blow to Liverpool's hopes that we might fall apart in our remaining fixtures.'

We were toughing it out to get results. At Arsenal, Gary was very fortunate not to be sent off along with Bobby Gould after a nasty clash in the opening minutes. There was tremendous rivalry between Leeds and Arsenal, which went back to the League Cup final at Wembley when there were some unsavoury clashes.

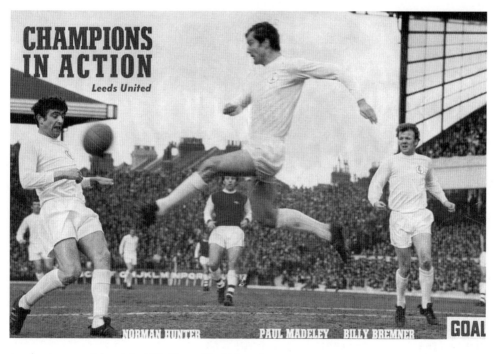

Leeds win a crucial match at Highbury, *Goal Magazine*.

Playing London teams was always extremely competitive, partly because the national press gave us a hard time. It did aggrieve us because we had some fantastic players. We were a very competitive side, but so were a lot of other teams – however, being the best side at the time in the country, everyone wanted to beat us. Every team had hard players in their side, and each week we'd come up against the likes of Dave Mackay, 'Chopper' Harris, Ron Yeats, Tommy Smith and Nobby Stiles. It wasn't easy, but if we had to mix it, we could. Naturally we preferred to play football, but at times we had to battle against some sides, and we had players capable of doing both.

On 22 April both Leeds and Liverpool drew their respective games 0-0. Leeds' stalemate at Everton meant they needed only a point for the title. Leeds returned to Merseyside on 28 April for an encounter with Liverpool that could decide the Championship race.

It was fitting that we had to play at Anfield, because they had been our main challengers all season. We had another game to go, but wanted to clinch the title on their ground. It was a really tough match. They had a few near misses and we also went close on a couple of

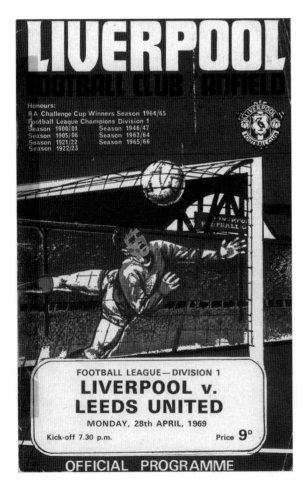

The last obstacle to the title!

Paul wins this aerial battle at Anfield in the title decider.

occasions, but we defended well and fully deserved our draw to win the League. We were all naturally ecstatic. Coming off the pitch, Don told us to salute the Kop. As we walked towards our great rival's fans and began to applaud them, suddenly they started chanting 'Champions, Champions...' and it got louder and louder. It was an amazing sight and sound. Bill Shankly put aside his personal disappointment and came into our dressing room after to congratulate us, which summed him up. He was a great personality.

Don Revie was jubilant: 'This is a fitting end to a wonderful season. The boys were magnificent tonight as they have been throughout the season. Winning the Championship makes me very glad for the players as well as the for rest of us ... All the team's fine character showed up last night. Liverpool came at us very hard and fast, but our men absorbed their effort like champions can, and then they gave as good as Liverpool had given. It would have been sweet to win the title at home, but if we had to win it away, then I am glad it has been done at Anfield. What a place to triumph at and what a crowd for generosity.'

Bill Shankly said: 'This is the greatest prize in football and Leeds deserve it. They have been a tremendously consistent side and tried so hard to win this Championship. There were two sets of champions in a great game tonight and a third set of champions emerged at the finish when the wonderful Liverpool fans showed the world what wonderful supporters they are.'

Billy Bremner added: 'We certainly played well tonight. We expected a hard game, and if you get a point here you have done well. We still have some critics, particu-

Champions! Champions! Leeds players take the applause from the Kop.

larly in the South, but I think our performances this season speak for themselves. You have to be a good team to win the league, and we have done that at last.'

Leeds United were the fourth Yorkshire club to win the Division One Championship. The media was unanimous in their praise.

Barry Foster, *Yorkshire Post*: 'It has taken the most consistent performance in the history of the League in the end to win the title, Leeds have recorded the fewest defeats ever in a First Division campaign, mainly due to the relentless way which Liverpool have tracked them. Last night, Liverpool's challenge ended when they failed to break down the Leeds defence which surpassed many of its famous feats in Europe in the way it shrugged off wave after wave of attacks...'

Derek Wallis, *Daily Mirror*: 'There has been no doubt in my mind for two seasons that Leeds are the best equipped of all English teams for the traps, tensions and special demands of the competition they will now enter – the European Cup. Leeds United are the Champions, the masters, the new kings of English football – at last.'

Donald Saunders, *Daily Telegraph*: 'Who could justly begrudge the dedicated, superbly efficient professionals from Elland Road their first success in this, the most demanding of all soccer competitions? Now, they have achieved their objective and earned nation-wide respect.'

Eric Todd, *Guardian*: 'The story of Leeds' remorseless march towards inevitable success could have been borrowed from the fiction section of any public library. But

A job well done...time to relax. Pictured are Jack Charlton, Paul Reaney, Gary Sprake, Johnny Giles, Paul, Peter Lorimer and Billy Bremner.

theirs is no fairy story. It is a real life epic of determination and dedication, the final chapters of which were written at Highbury, Goodison and now Anfield where Leeds, respectively, achieved victory and two draws. These performances in themselves merited the highest reward because Arsenal, Everton and Liverpool all were treading on Leeds' coat tails until recently. Never in all my intervening years have I seen any side subjected to such remorseless, pitiless pressure as were Leeds this night. Time after time it seemed that Leeds must crack, and time after time Liverpool were driven back by a defence, which has been the despair of so many teams in this country. Against an ordinary side Liverpool would have won, but then Leeds are not an ordinary side.'

Phil Brown, *Yorkshire Evening Post*: 'It was not a game for the faint hearted, but for all its fierceness it was sportingly played. In a season when bookings have been ten a penny, it was good to see this crucial match decently played, and the vast Anfield Kop give its own thunderous tribute at the end...that told United they deserved the point which had brought them their first Championship. The steely stuff of which Champions are made was easily seen in United as they delivered their quiet knockout blow.'

Two days later, Leeds played Nottingham Forest at Elland Road. Their 1-0 win created numerous records. Most points in a season (67), most home points (39), most wins (27), most home wins (18), fewest defeats (2), fewest away defeats (2), goals conceded (26) and goals conceded at home (9).

Leeds United League record: P42 W 27 D 13 L 2 F 66 A 26 Pts 67

Player appearances during the season (substitute in brackets): Sprake 42, Reaney 42, Cooper 34(1), Bremner 42, Charlton 41, Hunter 42, Lorimer 25(4), O'Grady 38, Jones 40, Giles 32, Gray 32(1), Madeley 31, Hibbitt 9(3), Belfitt 6(2), Bates 3(1), Greenhoff 3, Johanneson 0(1)

Goals: Jones 14, Lorimer 9, O'Grady 8, Giles 8, Bremner 6, Gray 5, Charlton 3, Madeley 3, Belfitt 3, Hibbitt 3, Johanneson 1, Cooper 1, Reaney 1, Own Goal 1

Paul Madeley had seen the club rise from Division Two minnows to champions since arriving as an apprentice.

A record-breaking match as Leeds set numerous records.

A perfect match ... Ann and Paul on their wedding day.

Winning the Championship was so satisfying, but what amazed me when we clinched the title at Anfield was the dressing room afterwards, because you just could not move. There were reporters; cameramen, every man and his dog seemed to be there. When you win a cup final, you expect all the hype, but not for a League game. It was quite strange and caught me by surprise, I thought we'd celebrate and then go home!

It was a great sense of achievement and the pinnacle for a player to be part of a Championship-winning team, because it's the standard everyone goes by. A cup triumph is a great occasion, but you only play a few intense games. In the League you play everyone, in all manner of conditions, and have to overcome injuries and suspensions. No one can argue that the best team comes out on top. Over a season bad decisions generally even themselves out, so there can be few complaints.

The atmosphere against Nottingham Forest was superb. It was a real party atmosphere, and of course the presentation of the trophy and civic reception, when thousands turned out, were all special moments. Two days later I married Ann. We decided not to have a big event, just a few relations. Although we didn't want the press to be present they managed to print a photograph in the Yorkshire Evening Post. *It had been some season!*

We are the Champions!

Yorkshire Evening Post cartoonist Speed's tribute to the new champs.

Chapter Six

TREBLE WOE

1969/70

Leeds were finally Champions, but Don Revie was not the type of manager to rest
on his laurels; he wanted to progress. Since taking over as manager in 1961 he had
taken the club from nowhere to the very pinnacle of English football. During pre-
season, Revie set his stall out for the new campaign by smashing the British record
transfer with the signing of Leicester City's Allan Clarke for £165,000. He wanted
Leeds to be able to challenge on all fronts and knew he needed a strike force and
squad capable of doing it. Pairing Clarke, renowned for his clinical finishing, with
Mick Jones was an inspirational decision.

*Although we had just won the title, we'd still not reached our peak: that was a couple of years
away. We feared nobody and were a formidable outfit. Don's decision to partner Mick with
Allan in attack offered the team a far greater outlet than when I was a 'makeshift' striker.
They were superb together and with Peter Lorimer in support caused every defence we came
up against problems.*

*Don always insisted on total commitment and Mick personified that. He was no 'fancy-
dan'. After arriving he soon fitted in. When Allan joined you could see from an early practice
game during pre-season that he would offer us a real cutting edge. I remember him glancing
in a couple of headers and tucking another chance away. It made me realise that we now had
the quality to round off the good work throughout the team.*

*During my early years Don had tried Jimmy Greenhoff and Rod Belfitt in attack, but
they both moved on. Jimmy had a lot of skill but lacked a bit of stamina, however he went
on to play for Stoke City and Manchester United and had some success. Similarly Rod was
a fine striker, but he wasn't the quickest of strikers, he went on to play for a number of clubs
including Ipswich Town.*

*Sometimes it boils down to small things. Two players can have equal ability, but if one is
half a yard quicker that can make all the difference at the top level. Without being disrespectful
to either Jimmy or Rod, Allan was a class act in front of goal and in a different league. He
was strong, quick and his finishing when one-on-one with a 'keeper was unbelievable. Allan
rarely missed and was so sharp in front of goal, which is how he got his nickname. During
the season Sam Leach, who presented Football Focus for the BBC's Grandstand programme,
was showing some of his goals on a show when he said that one of Allan's great strengths was
'sniffing out chances'. Well, of course we fell about laughing, but the nickname 'Sniffer' stuck.*

Leeds United, 1969/70. From left to right, back row: Revie (manager), Reaney, Hunter, Belfitt, Gray. Middle row: O'Grady, Charlton, Sprake, Harvey, Jones, Madeley. Front row: Clarke, Cooper, Hibbitt, Bremner (captain), Giles, Bates.

With Leeds entering the European Cup for the first time the team attracted mass media coverage. Journalist Eric Cooper questioned why Paul had still to win an England cap, insisting he was the one player who should be a certainty for England's World Cup squad. Even though he had no particular position to call his own, Cooper believed Madeley was good enough to stake a claim in a number of positions.

> Madeley plays like a man without a problem in the world or a football position to present any, yet whatever the role or the occasion his unflagging effort and ability are matched only by his impeccable behaviour.

Every aspect of the team's preparation was analysed. The *Daily Express* published a 26-hour timetable showing the players movements prior to a mid-week match!

Tuesday:
5.30 p.m. Team coach leaves Elland Road for a quiet hotel in the Yorkshire Dales
6.30 p.m. Dinner in reserved lounge
7.30 p.m. A spirited game of knockout carpet bowls, cup-style, at ten bob a head
9.00 p.m. Bingo session

10.00 p.m. Break for tea and biscuits

10.30 p.m. Les Cocker hands out training kit and players retire to twin-bedded rooms

Wednesday:

10.00 a.m. Tea and toast in bedrooms

11.00 a.m. Party leaves for half-hour training session

12.00 p.m. Back to hotel for shower

1.00 p.m. Lunch

2.00 p.m. Five houses of bingo

2.30 p.m. Tea and toast in bedrooms for rest

4.30 p.m. Pre-match tea

5.15 p.m. Party leaves hotel for Elland Road

6.00 p.m. Arrive at ground. Don Revie gives 45-minute team-talk in the players' lounge

6.45 p.m. Change for game

7.15 p.m. Referee checks studs and equipment

7.30 p.m. Kick off

The only downside of being a footballer was all the travelling. For years, before a game we stayed at the Craiglands Hotel in Ilkley. I shared with a number of the lads but mainly Mick Jones and David Harvey. Our pre-match build up included bingo and indoor bowls for many years. Pundits tended to knock this routine, but it worked for us and helped relax us. On coach journeys there were a number of card schools; I usually played with Mick, Norman and Terry. I found the travelling boring and never enjoyed it, so the cards really helped to pass the time. If we had a good result the return journey home always seemed quicker. For matches in London we tended to travel by train. Don organised a police escort to get us to Kings Cross. There was a fast train at 5.30 p.m. so we had to get away pretty sharp, but always just managed it and got back home at a reasonable time.

Leeds' first competitive game of the season was the Charity Shield where they entertained FA Cup holders Manchester City at Elland Road.

Leeds United v. Manchester City, Charity Shield

LEEDS UNITED: Sprake, Reaney, Cooper, Bremner (captain), Charlton, Hunter, Madeley, Clarke, Jones (Lorimer), Giles, Gray

MANCHESTER CITY: Corrigan, Book, Pardoe, Doyle, Booth, Oakes, Summerbee, Bell, Law, Young, Coleman

Following a 2-1 victory, Leeds began the defence of the Championship with a fine 3-1 win against Tottenham Hotspur.

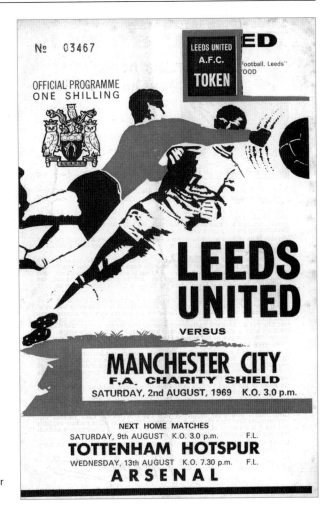

No 03467

**LEEDS UNITED
A.F.C.
TOKEN**

OFFICIAL PROGRAMME
ONE SHILLING

LEEDS UNITED

VERSUS

MANCHESTER CITY
F.A. CHARITY SHIELD
SATURDAY, 2nd AUGUST, 1969 K.O. 3.0 p.m.

NEXT HOME MATCHES
SATURDAY, 9th AUGUST   K.O. 3.0 p.m.   F.L.
TOTTENHAM HOTSPUR
WEDNESDAY, 13th AUGUST   K.O. 7.30 p.m.   F.L.
A R S E N A L

The season gets off to a flyer
with another trophy.

I played against some great stars; one was Tottenham's Jimmy Greaves who was always very complimentary in the Press about Leeds. Fortunately I didn't mark him too often! In the opening game we were 2-0 up when Jimmy got the ball just outside the box and sliced through our renowned defence, me included, rolled it round the 'keeper before tapping it in the corner. Sometimes certain players are just unstoppable – this was such an occasion. It was a sensational goal and you had to admire his talent. He was a class act; however, we went on to win 3-1.

Despite this confident start, Leeds' early form was patchy, winning only two of their opening six fixtures; though a 0-0 draw at Arsenal equalled Burnley's long-standing Division One record of 30 matches undefeated. Everton were the early pacesetters and ended Leeds' unbeaten run with a 3-2 at Goodison Park.

The defeat at Goodison was the wake-up call Leeds needed. Following a 2-1 victory at Sheffield Wednesday, Leeds won twelve out of their next sixteen matches to put them back in the title-race. The Clarke-Jones partnership was also developing

SECRETARY:
ALAN HARDAKER

THE FOOTBALL LEAGUE LIMITED

TELEPHONE:
ST. ANNES 22161-2-3-4

TELEX:
67675

ANY REPLY TO THIS LETTER
SHOULD BE ADDRESSED TO THE
SECRETARY. AND THE FOLLOWING
REFERENCE QUOTED

LYTHAM ST. ANNES
LANCS.
FY8 1JG

TELEGRAMS:
"LEAGUE" ST. ANNES

EH/PC/502   4 September, 1969

The Secretary,

......*Leeds United*............ Football Club

Dear Sir,

Re: International League Match
The Football League v.
The Football League of Ireland
at Barnsley on 10th September, 1969
Kick-off 7:30.p.m.
- - - - - - - - - - - - - - - - - -

Will you please intimate to ......*P. E. Madeley*......
that he has been selected to play in the above Match,
and inform him to report to Sir Alfred Ramsey at
Hallam Tower Hotel, Sheffield, by 9:00.p.m. on
MONDAY, 8th September, 1969.

Yours sincerely,

A. Hardaker

Secretary.

More representative honours … this time with the Football League XI.

fast; no team was safe. During a sensational run of results Nottingham Forest 6–1, Ipswich 4–0 and West Ham 4–1 were thumped; the Hammers triumph prior to Christmas finally clawing back Everton's eight–point advantage. The opening months of the season had seen Paul play left-back, centre-back and midfield. His performances were receiving rave reviews and journalists speculated whether he would make Sir Alf Ramsey's England squad.

In September 1969 Paul won his first representative honours when he played for the Football League in their 3–0 win over the League of Ireland. Three months later, Ramsey named a party of 30 players to face Portugal in a friendly international at Wembley. Seven Leeds players were included in the squad, including Paul for the first time.

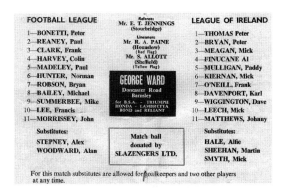

FOOTBALL LEAGUE	Referee: Mr. E. T. JENNINGS (Stourbridge)	LEAGUE OF IRELAND
1—BONETTI, Peter		1—THOMAS Peter
2—REANEY, Paul	Linesmen: Mr. R. A. PAINE (Hounslow) (Red Flag)	2—BRYAN, Peter
3—CLARK, Frank	Mr. S. ALLOTT (Sheffield) (Yellow Flag)	3—MEAGAN, Mick
4—HARVEY, Colin		4—FINUCANE Al
5—MADELEY, Paul	GEORGE WARD	5—MULLIGAN, Paddy
6—HUNTER, Norman	Doncaster Road Barnsley	6—KIERNAN, Mick
7—ROBSON, Bryan	for B.S.A. - TRIUMPH HONDA - LAMBRETTA BOND and RELIANT	7—O'NEILL, Frank
8—BAILEY, Michael		8—DAVENPORT, Karl
9—SUMMERBEE, Mike		9—WIGGINGTON, Dave
10—LEE, Francis		10—LEECH, Mick
11—MORRISSEY, John		11—MATTHEWS, Johnny
Substitutes: STEPNEY, Alex WOODWARD, Alan	Match ball donated by SLAZENGERS LTD.	Substitutes: HALE, Alfie SHEEHAN, Martin SMYTH, Mick

For this match substitutes are allowed for goalkeepers and two other players at any time.

Paul's in good company for this clash.

Don Revie was naturally delighted. Speaking to Peter Shaw of the *Sunday Mirror* Revie said: 'I was overjoyed to have seven players worthy of selection by Sir Alf, but there is no doubt that Paul Madeley's selection gave me that extra bit of pleasure. This is no reflection on the rest. It is just that Paul deserved this reward that little bit more for all his patience and loyalty. There were clubs willing to pay a lot of money for him and give him a regular first-team place, but how can you replace a player who can play so many positions so well. I couldn't let him go. Now I hope he feels it has all been worthwhile.'

Paul told reporters:

I read all over the place that I had a chance of a cap but I didn't take it seriously. I honestly didn't expect to make the squad against Portugal. It's certainly the nearest I've got to a cap but there is still a long way to go yet. After all only eleven can play on Wednesday. Obviously I hope to go to Mexico, but this is a step in the right direction.

As it transpired Paul failed to get a run out, however further speculation was mounting about his immediate future.

Interviewed by James Mossop, *Sunday Express,* Don Revie said:

I wouldn't part with him for a quarter of a million pounds; I haven't a price. If Paul had a permanent position I feel he would have had international recognition by now. He is a wonderful lad to have around. Wherever I ask him to play, he just nods his head and says 'Right'. The other players here call him 'Mr Ed', after television's talking horse that says very little. We don't get much conversation out of him. He comes here, says 'Good morning', stays at the forefront of training and goes home just as quietly as he came. I remember the first time I saw him. It was a Sunday afternoon and the Leeds juniors were playing a team from the Leeds and District FA. Our scout, Jack Breedon, had told me to keep an eye on their left-half. It was Paul. I stood on the touchline and was immediately struck by the graceful way he was able to glide past opponents. I reckoned that if we could sharpen him up with professional training we might be able to develop him; though I never anticipated he would turn out to be so good.

As for Madeley, he told local reporters:

I don't mind being a play-anywhere man, I am just happy to get a game. A lot of people seem to think I will automatically take over at centre-half from Jack Charlton, but the big man has a few years left in him yet. Besides, the role I enjoy most of all is the one I am playing at the moment – midfield. My aspect is mainly defensive, and I do like to get back. Being there means that I can do the covering while Billy Bremner and Johnny Giles express themselves. I'm a professional and play where I'm selected. I realise that many of the other lads would be prepared to switch around too if the boss wanted them. That's the way we've been brought up at Leeds. We're a team and I'm part of that team no matter where they pick me to play. I've played in nearly every position except goalkeeper for United, but I've no regrets. In fact it's one of the reasons I was chosen as Player of the Year by our supporters a few years ago. I'm very proud of that honour, and proud to play for Leeds anywhere they want me.

As New Year approached, although out of the League Cup (losing 2-0 to Chelsea), Leeds were going well in their defence of the League and were through to the latter

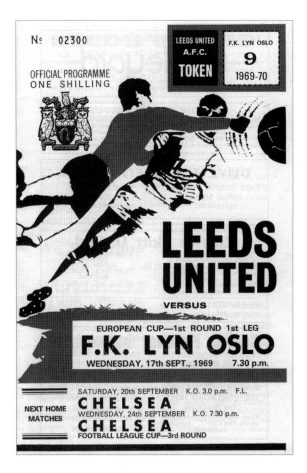

Leeds hit 10 on their
European Cup bow.

stages of the European Cup. The first round brought a club record 10-0 win (16-0 on aggregate) against amateurs SK Lyn Oslo from Norway.

The media felt sorry for the Norwegians. Alan Thompson, *Daily Express*: 'It was all so easy, this merciless hammering and it could have been many more.'

Before the game Don tried to boost the crowd by telling supporters we were going for a record score, but as the game went on you couldn't help but feel a bit sorry for the opposition.

In the second round Leeds faced Ferencvaros, but the predicted classic never materialised. Leeds dominated both legs, winning both 3-0 for a 6-0 aggregate win. The victory was historic, as they became the first British team to win in Hungary's Nep Stadium. The quarter-finals scheduled for March paired Leeds with Standard Liege.

Back on the domestic front, Leeds beat league leaders Everton 2-1. The win began another unbeaten run, which included a hard-fought draw with Liverpool at Elland Road and revenge over Sheffield Wednesday following their cup defeat the previous season. There had also been impressive victories against Chelsea 5-2 and West Brom 5-1.

By now Leeds were also through to the FA Cup quarter-finals having beaten Swansea, Sutton and Mansfield. Paul missed this latter match, which is unbelievably the only occasion Don Revie's world famous XI – Sprake, Reaney, Cooper, Bremner, Charlton, Hunter, Lorimer, Clarke, Jones, Giles and Gray – played a professional match together. The reason ... Paul Madeley was always in the side.

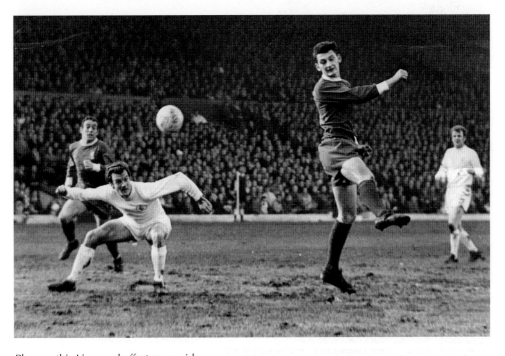

Phew ... this Liverpool effort goes wide.

Paul loses out, but Leeds defeat
Sheffield Wednesday 2-0.

Close call ... Swindon 'keeper Peter Downsborough and Paul both miss a cross during a hard-fought cup-tie.

This fact still amazes me. Everyone knows the 'great' side, but incredibly they only played one game together, which is quite unbelievable. It's bizarre, but I can fully understand it. If I were to name the great Don Revie team, I would also name this XI ... and not include myself because the other players had a set position, I didn't.

However, someone was normally carrying a knock and when a player regained fitness, someone else was out. Also, Don often changed tactics for certain games and many times he'd ask me to man-mark someone. I always played and expected to play. I would have been disappointed if I wasn't picked.

At the beginning of March the treble was still a distinct possibility for Leeds, but after their opening quarter-final leg with Standard Liege serious fixture congestion was looming. One of the first games was a humdinger at Liverpool and it's a match Paul recalls only too well because of the goal that never counted...

One of the highlights of the season were our clashes with Liverpool. There was a huge rivalry, but both clubs also had tremendous respect for each other. Throughout my career, Anfield was my favourite ground. Running out under the famous 'Welcome to Anfield' sign always inspired me to perform and was very special. It was a tremendous venue to play at and their supporters created a fantastic atmosphere, which intimidated opponents, and most teams struggled, but we didn't see it that way. We had some terrific battles over the years; fortunately we seemed to win the crucial ones.

There was snow on the ground for this game. It was freezing cold but the referee passed the pitch playable. It was a typical Leeds v Liverpool clash, really tight with few opportunities. I was playing the anchor role in midfield, but in the dying seconds of the game, with the score 0-0, I foraged forward, played a one-two against Ron Yeats' boots and stuck it in the corner past Ray Clemence. I ran off to celebrate, but when I turned round all the other players were walking off the pitch, I couldn't believe it. I looked across at Ray and he was beating the ground in frustration. We were the only two who had not heard the final whistle from the referee!

In the FA Cup, Leeds faced their great rivals Manchester United – the tie would become a marathon...

Following the Hillsborough clash, Geoffrey Green of *The Times* commented: 'They say they (Leeds) relish hard work, that the expense of energy seems an eternal delight. But surely there must be a limit.'

Tom Holley, *Yorkshire Evening Post*, added, 'this was the result Don Revie did not want.'

After another titanic battle in the first replay, Alan Thompson in the *Daily Express* observed: 'Even defeat might have tasted sweeter to Leeds than this draw. A second replay was the last thing they want because of a demanding fixture congestion that is already heavily congested.'

Finally, Leeds' fighting spirit defeated their Pennine rivals thanks to a terrific strike from Billy Bremner.

I played midfield during the game at Hillsborough, but reverted to defence for the other matches after Norman picked up a knock. I man-marked Bobby Charlton. He was a terrific

My ball … Paul is on hand as Gary
Sprake safely gathers during a
gripping second replay against
Manchester United.

Wembley here we come!

player and had a great knack of making space for himself, a quick feint and he was gone. It was always a challenge. They had some great stars. Fortunately, I never came across Denis Law a great deal, but Norman had some tussles with him, and George Best was something special when on song.

Both teams were desperate to win, and at times we had to defend valiantly. They were really tough battles. In the first replay we were fortunate to get away with the draw because they missed a couple of glorious chances, but that's cup football and we made them pay in the second replay when Billy struck the winning goal early on. We were naturally all delighted, especially after losing consecutive semi-finals. For a number of us this would be our first FA Cup final, so it was an extremely satisfying victory.

In the midst of the FA Cup trilogy, Leeds overcame Liege 2-0 on aggregate to reach the European Cup semi-finals. However, having battled through two replays in the space of four days they now faced five games in eight days, including a European Cup semi-final against Celtic ... Something had to give ...

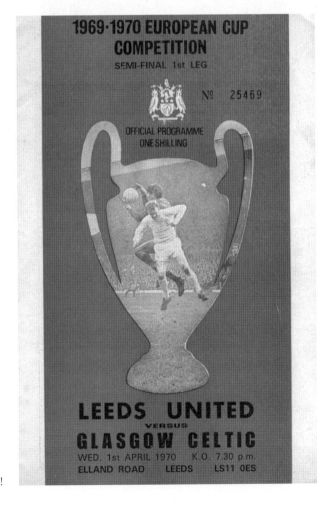

The Scots come to town!

All eyes on the ball as Connelly (partially hidden behind Terry Cooper) grabs Celtic an early lead at Elland Road.

With players mentally and physically fatigued Revie rested players, signalling an end to Leeds' title defence. Following a 3-1 defeat at home to Southampton on 28 March, Tom German of *The Times* wrote: 'If they (Leeds) lose the Championship, it is because of commitments heaped on them by the rewards of their own talents.' As Leeds prepared for their semi-final clash Revie fielded a second string against Derby, an act that brought a media backlash and a fine from the Football Association!

When Leeds ran out to face Celtic, only a few days had passed since booking their Cup Final slot, and it showed in the players' performance as Leeds lost 1-0. A visitor at the Celtic clash was Liverpool boss Bill Shankly, who had only sympathy for Leeds.

> Chelsea could win the FA Cup final... but they are not in the same class as Leeds United... Everton have won the League Championship while the best team this country has seen for a long time is in a position where it might win nothing... this has been a vicious season for Leeds. The whole world has come down on them. Celtic were healthy and strong, Leeds were not... They had faced too many injuries and too many games. If Leeds are beaten in the Cup Final it will complete a tragic season for them.

> *With all the games, mentally we lost a bit of edge. It certainly cost us against Celtic when they scored early on in the first leg at Elland Road.*

Twenty-four hours after the Celtic defeat, Leeds faced West Ham. Revie played six regulars, but for Paul Reaney it proved a disaster. A broken leg ended his season and World Cup dreams. Two days later Leeds faced Burnley. Only Madeley, Lorimer and Gray played from the first team, but Leeds' 2-1 win is still remembered for Eddie Gray's 'goal in a million'.

Reaney's loss was not lost on Revie, who took the opportunity to stress the value of his star utility player. 'People get agog about Paul Madeley's ability to play in different positions that they tend to forget he's a world-class player. However, you cannot exaggerate his value. Having him at the club is like having three men in one. He can do any job. Paul just goes out and does exactly what you want him to do; I never need to worry about him.'

With a week to prepare for the Cup Final the Leeds players relaxed before their showdown with Chelsea. However, Reaney's misfortune brought ramifications not only for Leeds but also Paul Madeley. Naturally he would replace his teammate at Wembley, but Sir Alf Ramsey now needed a replacement in his 28-man World Cup squad, of which Reaney was a member. His choice was Madeley who heard the news via *Daily Mail* reporter Bill Mallinson. Madeley's comments appeared the following day in the *Mail*, just three days before the Cup Final.

You must be joking, it just isn't possible. I had just disregarded the World Cup altogether when I was not originally included in the reserves... it's incredible really. I seem to get my chance through other people's misfortunes, especially those of my own teammates. But, I'm still keeping my fingers crossed because the 28 have to be reduced to 22 before the tournament starts.

Within 24 hours though Paul had shocked Ramsey and Football Authorities by pulling out of the pre-tournament trip. The Football Association issued an official

The 'Magnificent Seven'. The Leeds players chosen for England's 'provisional' World Cup squad in 1970. From left to right: Terry Cooper, Paul Reaney, Mick Jones, Norman Hunter, Paul Madeley, Allan Clarke and Jack Charlton.

statement. 'Paul Madeley has withdrawn for personal reasons and because he is very tired because of the number of matches he has played this season.'

Speaking to the *Yorkshire Evening Post* through Don Revie, Paul's gave his reasons. 'I am very tired, and feel I would do neither England nor myself full football justice if I did not withdraw from Mexico.'

Revie was sympathetic to his player, understanding better that anyone the physical and mental stress his players were going through as the season reached its climax. 'It was a great opportunity for him, but he feels he has had such a hard season that what he needs is a good holiday for himself and his wife. This is typical of Paul, an honest player who isn't concerned about the money he would have earned (around £10,000) but more about his own efforts with the England team.'

Madeley's replacement Bob McNab of Arsenal failed to make the 22-man squad for the finals in Mexico ...

I've never changed my view on this subject; I made the right decision at the time. Sir Alf called up a number of players during the season in his preparation for the World Cup finals. I was called into a few squads, and made his original World Cup squad of 40, along with seven Leeds players, but got dropped when it was cut to 28 players. The remaining 12 players were placed on standby

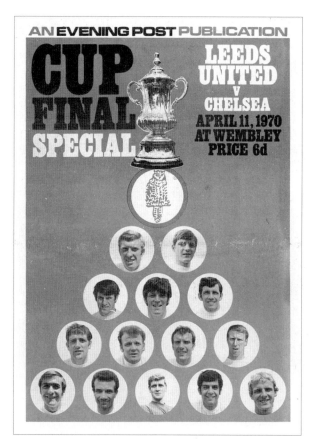

Yorkshire Evening Post FA
Cup final special.

whilst the 28-man squad was eventually reduced to 22 after the post-season tour. The six players missing out had the choice of joining the party as a non-playing member or could return home.

When Paul Reaney broke his leg, I was promoted to the squad of 28 players, but decided to turn it down. Just to travel and watch did not make sense at the time. I was flattered to be in the 28-man squad, however I felt I'd be going along for the ride with no chance of making the final 22. I discussed my feelings with Don and told him I'd be better resting up after the long season and be fresh for the new campaign. He understood my feelings and arranged for the club to put out an official statement. The papers slated me, and slanted it that I'd snubbed England, which was not the case at all. I couldn't believe the amount of publicity that I received.

I watched England's defence of the World Cup along with the rest of the country on television. At the time I felt that I'd never be picked for another England squad, but it wasn't held against me. Alf never talked to me about it and called me up the following season. I went on to win 24 caps, which I'm extremely proud of.

Come Cup Final day, all the talk in the media centred on the atrocious playing surface caused by The Horse of the Year Show and incessant rain in London. Despite the conditions, Leeds summoned all their reserves of energy to shine at Wembley.

Leeds United, 1970 FA Cup final squad. From left to right, back row: Reaney, Sprake, Harvey, Cooper. Middle row: Bremner (captain), Hunter, Charlton, Madeley, Yorath. Front row: Gray, Lorimer, Giles, Bates, Clarke, Jones, Hibbitt, Belfitt.

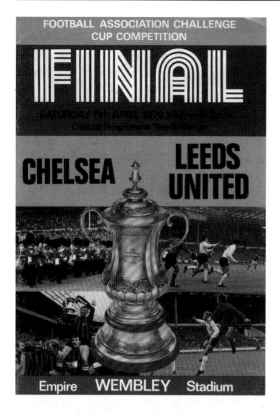

A Wembley classic!

Chelsea v. Leeds United, FA Cup final:

CHELSEA: Bonetti, Webb, McCreadie, Hollins, Dempsey, Harris (captain) (Hinton), Baldwin, Houseman, Osgood, Hutchison, Cooke

LEEDS UNITED: Sprake, Madeley, Cooper, Bremner (captain), Charlton, Hunter, Lorimer, Clarke, Jones, Giles, Gray

A pulsating encounter ended in a 2-2 draw resulting in a replay for the first time in 58 years. Reporters had witnessed an unforgettable match.

Geoffrey Green wrote: 'It was not a classic but an epic … the finest final seen at Wembley since the war … it had everything from A to Z'.

Barry Foster, *Yorkshire Post*: 'After all their efforts this season it will be something of an injustice if Leeds United finish empty handed, yet Leeds still have to produce the knock-out blow … Leeds set Wembley alight with one of their extra-special displays … They used the wide-open spaces of Wembley with great control and accuracy despite sand-covered stretches, which played havoc with the bounce, and speed of the ball.'

Don Revie was proud of his players: 'We showed everybody we can still play, I've never seen them play better. I don't think we'll hear any more about unattractive Leeds after today!'

Above: Don Revie and Dave Sexton lead their teams out at Wembley.

Right: Final formalities ... Paul waits in line to meet H.R.H. Princess Anne.

Leeds clear the danger during a 'Twin Towers' thriller.

Big Jack nods Leeds in front at Wembley. Paul's on hand but the ball crossed over the line.

By Cup Final day we were rested and ready. I recall going for an early morning stroll with Mick on the morning of the match and we were both really looking forward to the game. On the day we played superbly. Big Jack gave us the lead before Gary's blunder before half-time from Houseman's daisy-cutter. We still thought we'd win and dominated play.

When Mick glided one in late on I thought that would be it, but you have to give them credit for coming back. Late on we were in Chelsea's half when I had an option to square the ball to Billy, but I decided to play a different pass, which was the wrong choice because they picked up the ball. Big Jack gave away a free kick and they scored the equaliser. That said we should have won because we dominated so much, but their heads never dropped and they battled away. Eddie Gray was superb, he roasted David Webb on the left-wing and had a fantastic match on a terrible surface. By the end both teams had settled for a replay, but in the dressing room afterwards we could not believe we hadn't won, however we were confident we'd win the replay at Old Trafford.

In a season that had stretched the team to its physical and mental limits, Leeds flew to Scotland for their second leg semi-final clash with Celtic. A record attendance of 136,500 crammed into Hampden Park.

We gave everything and when Billy scored a brilliant 35-yarder it was game on, but they came back strong and won 3-1 on aggregate in the end. Overall they were the better side, but I'd loved to have faced them when we fully fit. It would have been some match.

All that now remained for Revie's team was the FA Cup ...

Chelsea v. Leeds United, FA Cup final replay:

CHELSEA: Bonetti, Harris (captain), McCreadie, Hollins, Dempsey, Webb, Baldwin, Cooke, Osgood (Hinton), Hutchison, Houseman
LEEDS UNITED: Sprake, Madeley, Cooper, Bremner (captain), Charlton, Hunter, Lorimer, Clarke, Jones, Giles, Gray

Leeds were refreshed after two weeks' rest, but Chelsea had also regrouped and changed their formation to combat Eddie Gray, switching Ron Harris with David Webb. Once again Mick Jones gave Leeds the lead but Chelsea battled back with headers from Peter Osgood and, in a cruel twist, David Webb scored an extra-time winner.

The media were universal in their sympathy for Leeds.

One reporter wrote: 'In any other walk of life you could get 20 years for robbery. In football if you're Chelsea you rob Leeds of their rightful possession of the FA Cup. Just how they did it is beyond my comprehension.'

Geoffrey Green summed up the match: 'One with vicious tackling – Boadicea might have been on parade'.

Don Revie, though choked, vowed: 'We will start again next season.'

Cup Final epic ... Part II.

We had our opportunities after Mick scored a super goal. I was particularly disappointed with their equalising goal because Peter Osgood managed to nip in between Norman and myself. Between the two of us we didn't mark him and it gave them impetus. You have to give them credit though and for David Webb to score the winner, well it was just incredible after the way Eddie tormented him at Wembley. Without making excuses, we lacked sharpness through these crucial games. You can do the running about, but mentally and physically your sharpness was hard to sustain over a long period of time.

Looking back, at least we were involved right to the end. Even though we didn't win the trophies we may have deserved over the years, and the disappointments were enormous at times, the club was buzzing. It was a great period for us. Every season we were involved in one tournament or another. Often pundits said we should concentrate on a specific tournament, but it just wasn't possible. Even the League Cup, which had a reputation for being a secondary competition domestically, you didn't go out consciously thinking let's not try.

Players were rested for certain matches, but that's why you had a squad. When other players came in, the team tried all they could to win. It's only when you've been knocked out that you subconsciously think, right we can concentrate on the League. As a player you wanted to win trophies, even though of course some had more prestige than others did. Its hard not to go for the win, and the farther you go in the competition the more that you want to win it. We may have missed out but what a season. How many players would have swapped their season for ours!

Final instructions before extra time from the boss ... but it wasn't to be.

Chapter Seven

DODGY DECISIONS AND WATERLOGGED PITCHES

1970/71

Following a well-deserved rest, Paul returned for pre-season training, the disappointments of the previous campaign consigned to history.

There was no feeling sorry for ourselves after missing out the previous term; we were all the more determined to win more trophies. I felt refreshed and knew my decision not to attend the World Cup was the correct one for me at the time. I enjoyed watching the finals but was ready to go again. As usual I'd kept myself in reasonable shape playing a fair bit of tennis, so pre-season training wasn't too bad, but it was hard work. Unlike some of the players I never had to shed any weight. Norman Hunter and myself always had a bet who would put more weight on. I'm still waiting for my pay out!

Leeds got off to a flying start, winning their opening five games before a stalemate against Arsenal. Leeds went out of the League Cup at the first round to Sheffield United, but in the Madeley household there was celebrations following the birth of their first son on 17 October.

Jason arrived the day we played Manchester United at home. I was designated to man-mark George Best that day, he had a blinder in a 2-2 draw.

Consistent performances kept Leeds in the mix, the only downside being the occasional gaffe from Gary Sprake, which cost vital goals. There had been the infamous own goal at Liverpool in 1966 when Sprake threw the ball into his own net, prompting supporters to sing *Careless Hands*, and following his Cup Final mistake against Chelsea, a last-minute lapse at Crystal Palace would cost another win. It did not effect the team though, following the clash at Selhurst Park, Leeds won six out of their next eight fixtures. During this spell Paul scored four goals playing at left-back, including for the second (and last) in his career three in consecutive matches!

The first was a header against Blackpool, before strikes against Stoke City and Wolves. Again I received some good-natured stick in the dressing room. 'Goal a Game Madeley' was back! Two weeks later I grabbed another at Anfield in a fine 1-1 draw from a Terry Cooper cross, which was very pleasing having had a goal disallowed the previous season. This would be my most prolific spell as a goal-scorer. It was nice whilst it lasted!

Leeds United, 1970/71. From left to right, back row: Galvin, Yorath, Harvey, Jones, Sprake, Charlton, Clarke, Hunter, Gray, Madeley. Front row: Belfitt, Reaney, Lorimer, Giles, Bremner (captain), Cooper, Bates, Hibbitt.

Goal! Paul powers in a header against Blackpool.

Paul signs autographs following a charity match at Throstles Nest, near Farsley. Proceeds benefited Airedale and Wharfedale Society for the mentally handicapped.

The 3-2 win at Wolves had journalists eulogising over one man's performance, with Derek Wallis, *Daily Mirror* advocating an international opportunity for the Leeds man.

Paul Madeley has skill, temperament, and knowledge to become one of modern football's great players. The trouble with being Paul Madeley is that he is such a complete footballer that he is widely regarded as just a useful player with a flair for improvisation. He is also thought of as a bit of a rebel because he refused the command of Sir Alf Ramsey to join him in Mexico. He is neither.

He may have jeopardised his immediate international future by not answering Ramsey's call, but that should not make him a Mexican bandit who ought to be outlawed for all time. This handsome giant of a man, whose ability to play in midfield, in defence or even in attack, has tended to obscure his immense talent, gave a vivid illustration in this match of his command of a wide range of techniques that make him an invaluable, even priceless player.

Madeley also confirmed that his most effective position is in midfield, where his perceptive performance, his ability to win the ball aggressively within the rules and his damaging distribution irritated Wolves to the point of distraction.

Despite his conspicuous frame, Madeley was able to steal unobtrusively into positions from which he could create the sort of situation from which all three Leeds goals came.

Madeley had contributed more than one man's share to the match already, but manager Don Revie had another assignment for him in the second half. He was withdrawn, not into the thick of the defence, but in front of it with instructions to intercept all moves. His presence thereafter was important to Leeds (leading 3-2). Attacks were repelled, sometimes wildly but mostly convincingly, and Leeds survived to control the game and collect two more points that makes their position at the summit even more secure.

After several seasons' recognition as the best all-rounder in the game, Don Revie was not disagreeing with Wallis' assessment. The Leeds boss was convinced that Madeley had the attributes to become one of the great players of world football. 'Paul's control and confidence have really blossomed during the past eighteen months. Physically he has the build of that perfectly built footballer John Charles. Technically it is almost impossible to fault him. The mark of many great players was that they operated for thirty minutes in bursts. This man operates for ninety minutes. When you put all his assets together he must, even now, be near enough the complete player.'

The accolades coincided with Paul playing the anchor role of the midfield three.

Playing in midfield with Billy Bremner and Johnny Giles was great. They seemed so natural as a partnership from the beginning and complemented each other so well. My role was straightforward. I was the anchorman to protect the back four, and after winning the ball would serve it up to either of them. It was an easy job really, I didn't need to think about playing a through ball; I was content to give it to the masters. However, I did have licence to move through, and I exercised this whenever possible.

It was wonderful to play behind them in midfield, they were both so capable on the ball. Their control and vision was amazing. They were both so aware of what they would do with the ball, before they received it. I spent a lot of my career marking out the danger man of the other side, which was very satisfying when you do it right, but not nearly as much as being able to express yourself, which arose when the opposition concentrated their attentions on Billy or John. Playing this role gave me some of my best memories as a player.

Leeds remained unbeaten until the New Year when Tottenham defeated them 2-1 at Elland Road; only their second defeat of the campaign. After wins over West Ham and Manchester City, the team embarked on another spell unbeaten as the chase for the title continued. Following the win over City, Alan Thompson in the *Sunday Express* singled out Paul's display and advocated an England call-up:

We have known for a long time what Leeds can do in the absence of diverse English, Welsh and Irish internationals, and we know what Leeds can do without one third of the Scottish national side. What I would like to know is how they would go on without their one non-international among their regular first team. Is there a more complete, consistent all-round footballer, or a cleaner, fairer opponent in the country today?

I am sorry to have to drag Sir Alf Ramsey into this, but how can he afford to leave the man out of his calculations is to me unfathomable. The man is Paul Madeley and he is neither one thing nor the other. Neither a forward, nor a defender, nor a midfield man … but what a player!

The thought has been with me for some time that in any given match he is worth three men to Leeds. In the space of 10 minutes on Saturday, Madeley did the lot. With assistance from Mick Bates he cleaved Manchester City in two, a minute later he was calmly taking the ball off Colin Bell, which is always an achievement, in his own goal-mouth. And when Jack Charlton went off with a broken nose, Madeley slotted into the centre-half position, the substitute came on and no way was the efficiency of the side impaired.

This surely is one of the great reasons for Leeds United's smoothness. When Madeley is about they can play the other men in their rightful positions, and when Madeley is about no one seems like a fish out of water.

Away from the race for the Championship, the team was going well in both the Fairs Cup and FA Cup. Leeds began their European campaign by overcoming Sarpsborg 6-0 on aggregate, before edging past Dynamo Dresden on away goals. An emphatic 9-2 aggregate win over Sparta Prague meant Leeds were once again challenging on three fronts. The FA Cup had seen victories over Rotherham and Swindon Town, which set up a fifth-round clash against a Fourth Division side Colchester United, but Leeds went into the clash on the back of a 1-0 defeat at home to Liverpool, another game when Paul had a goal disallowed.

The Liverpool loss soon paled into insignificance following arguably the biggest shock in FA Cup history when the underdogs beat Don Revie's mighty Leeds side.

Leeds defence close in on Sparta Prague forward Masek to deny the danger-man a strike at goal.

Another strike from Paul against Liverpool is chalked off, this time due to a foul by Clarke.

Hunter grabs a goal, but it's too late to prevent one of the biggest FA Cup shocks ever ... Colchester 3 Leeds 2.

Barry Foster, *Yorkshire Post* was stunned: 'A side as superstitious as Leeds might have known something extraordinary was on the cards on the 13th of the month, but to be the giant in the biggest giant-killing act since Jack and the Beanstalk was a terrible blow to take.'

No excuses, they deserved their win. The pitch was poor though, that said we had enough class in the side. Apart from Billy everyone was there, it was a big disappointment but that's what the FA Cup is all about and why it is so special. Tactically we made mistakes, which was unusual for us. Don mistakenly thought that due to the bumpy pitch we'd be unable to play our normal passing game. We gave the ball away a lot and consequently suffered. We were indecisive at the back and found ourselves 3-0 down, which no one could quite believe. We came back with goals from Norman and John when we played our regular game, knocking the ball about, but it was too late. We ran out of time for one of the great cup shocks. The papers had a field day the following morning!

Leeds bounced back with four consecutive wins, including one against Wolves in which Paul scored his fifth goal of the season. With only eight League games remaining Leeds had a six-point lead over their only challengers Arsenal, who had two games in hand.

Vitoria Setubal defender Rebolo clears his lines as Leeds search for a winner.

Billy's header gives Leeds
an edge in the opening leg.

Back in Europe, Leeds overcame a quarter-final clash against the crack Portuguese side Vitoria Setubal. The team's 3-2 aggregate win set up a semi-final 'clash of the giants' between the best two sides in England, Leeds and Liverpool. Following a defeat at Chelsea, Burnley were beaten 4-0, however, nerves were becoming frayed after draws against Newcastle and Huddersfield Town. There was no time to rest though as Leeds faced Liverpool in the Fairs Cup. Don Revie recalled Billy Bremner, who had been struggling with an injury for a number of months, for the first leg at Anfield and it paid off.

Billy was such an inspirational player, he'd been out for months but came back as if he'd never been away. Once again he came up trumps in a major semi-final, but it had been mighty close.

Buoyed by their win at Anfield, a League-Fairs Cup 'double' was a real possibility when Leeds ran out to face West Brom, a side without an away win in sixteen months. *Match of the Day* covered the game and was now analysing key moments from a match with slow motion replays. Ray Tinkler refereed the clash...

We'd been going well and the title race was between Arsenal and ourselves. West Brom was a really key game because although Arsenal were catching us we were in control of our own destiny. I'd played every League game up to this match, but fell ill on the morning of the match at the Craiglands Hotel during our preparation. I got a taxi home and waited to hear the result.

The match, which Leeds lost 2-1 changed the course of the title race and has become one of the most infamous games in the club's history. West Brom's second goal by Jeff Astle proved pivotal in the game and three decades on is one of the most talked about incidents of the era. At the time, everybody was talking about the game; Don Revie went on television to debate the incident and commented bitterly that 'nine months hard work was down the drain by a referee's decision'. As for the referee, he was adamant that the player involved in the incident (Colin Suggett) was not 'interfering with play' therefore there was no need to whistle. Tinkler had few supporters.

I saw the game later on television and could not believe the offside goal that was given. When Tony Brown intercepted Norman Hunter's pass and began to break away across the halfway line; the linesman immediately raised his flag because Colin Suggett was yards offside. Even Brown stopped, but unbelievably Tinkler waved play on. Brown carried the ball forward before squaring it to Jeff Astle to score. The crowd went wild. What upset them so much was clearly the goal but also the fact that we'd just had an equaliser from Mick Jones harshly disallowed. What I recall most was Don Revie's face as he looked up at the sky whilst walking off the pitch

Leeds fans invade the pitch following West Brom's controversial 'offside' goal.

Leeds attack in the second leg in a classic against Liverpool in Europe.

after the pitch invasion. He knew how costly the referee's decision could prove. You work so hard to achieve things, and to miss out because of a decision like that was scandalous. When I saw the lads on the Monday, they were still devastated.

Although we won our final League games of the season, it was not enough. Arsenal pipped us by a point. I know the best team invariably comes out on top during a League campaign, and 'bad' decisions even out over the course of a season, but without detracting anything from Arsenal, the second goal in the West Brom clash cost us the title. One can only imagine what the media today, with all the television cameras available, would have made of that goal. At the time it was a bitter pill to take, and took some getting over.

For Leeds United, the season was not quite over just yet. One prize still remained to be won – the Fairs Cup. In a gruelling battle, both Clarke and Jones went off injured but a resilient defence snuffed out Liverpool's attack to send Leeds through to a second Fairs Cup final in four years. With a cup final to look forward to, Paul finally won a first England cap when he was picked to face Northern Ireland in the Home International Championships. His ascent to full international status made him the 13th player on the clubs books with full honours and made Revie's first team an all-international XI. He might have backed out of the World Cup finals, but that was now history. Media reaction to his elevation was unanimous... not before time Sir Alf!

Northern Ireland v. England, Home International Championships

ENGLAND: Banks (Stoke City), Madeley (Leeds United), Cooper (Leeds United), Storey (Arsenal), McFarland (Derby County), Moore (West Ham, captain), Lee (Manchester City), Ball (Everton), Chivers (Tottenham Hotspur), Clarke (Leeds United), Peters (Tottenham Hotspur)

I joked with reporters that Alf had finally forgiven me for turning down Mexico! I must admit, I never really expected to get back into the international squad so it was a big surprise when I was picked to play against Northern Ireland. I had the unenviable task of marking George Best. He was an unbelievable talent; fortunately he switched flanks after a few minutes. During the game, I remember him scoring a really 'cheeky' goal that was disallowed and created some debate. Gordon Banks was about to clear the ball upfield when George kicked the ball from his hands and popped the ball in. The referee may have disallowed it, but I remember thinking we were lucky to get away with it because Gordon didn't have control of the ball. The Irish players felt especially hard done by when Allan scored the only goal of the match, because he did look suspiciously offside.

Don Revie was determined that his team should not end the season empty handed. He knew it would be tough though, because his team was facing the mighty Juventus. Speaking with reporters during the build-up to the first leg in Turin, Revie promised his team would be trying 'harder over the next two matches than they have ever done in the ten years I've been in charge.'

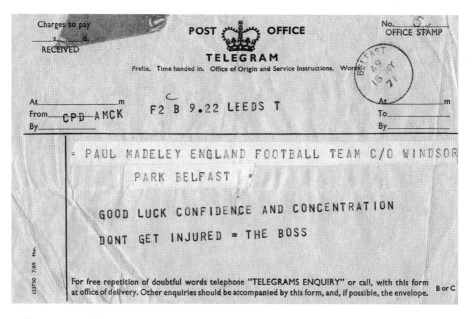

Full international honours at last!

England, 1971 Home International squad. From left to right, back row: Shilton, Smith, Lloyd, Nish, Lawler, Brown, Hughes, McFarland, Clemence, Banks, Moore, Peters, Chivers. Front row: Madeley, Coates, Clarke, Cooper, Hurst, Kidd, Storey, Ball, Lee, Harvey.

Juventus v. Leeds United, 1971 Fairs Cup final first leg:

JUVENTUS: Piloni, Spinosi, Marchetti, Furino, Morino, Salvadore, Haller, Causio, Anastasi (Novellini), Capello, Bettaga

LEEDS UNITED: Sprake, Reaney, Cooper, Bremner (captain), Charlton, Hunter, Lorimer, Clarke, Jones (Bates), Giles, Madeley

In a sensational game, full of entertaining football, Leeds twice came from behind to cancel out goals from the Juventus millionaire forward line. The pressure at times was relentless, but the defence succeeded in masterly fashion. Barry Foster of the *Yorkshire Post* said that Leeds' performance at the Stadio Comunle was one of the 'finest displays of courage, enlightened football and determination' he had witnessed.

Don Warters of the *Yorkshire Evening Post* was privileged to witness this epic encounter. 'It was a proud Leeds United who prepared to fly home from Turin today, basking, and deservedly so, in the glory of yet another enthralling display, which makes them hot favourites to carry off the Fairs Cup again. Rarely does one have the opportunity of seeing such a tremendous match, and Juventus played a full part in an entertaining spectacle. The final half hour in particular was packed with football, which will not be easily forgotten, and the teams went in determinedly at each other in an all-out effort to gain a first leg advantage.'

For Paul, the first leg would be particularly memorable as he scored one of the crucial away goals. His fourth and final goal in European competition would also be his only goal in a major cup final.

Juventus had a superb side, with a number of world-class stars, but we were not overawed. We were experienced in Europe and knew we could give them a game. The conditions were appalling because it had rained from the moment we arrived in Turin. Within minutes of the kick off there was a torrential storm, which made it a lottery. A number of times their players were bouncing the ball in puddles saying there was no way they could carry on. The referee eventually abandoned the game early in the second half. We went back to the hotel and replayed the game two days later.

As it transpired Juventus did us a favour because the 2-2 draw gave us the edge with two away goals. It was one of our best-ever away performances in Europe and somewhat surprisingly both Mick Bates and myself scored our goals. Between the two of us we only scored a handful of goals in Europe so it was pretty amazing that we both scored in a European final. My goal was a long-range speculative daisy-cutter. I hit it quite well, but it just clipped a defender some distance from me, which wrong-footed the 'keeper completely.

Two weeks later Leeds lined up determined to end the season with something to show for their efforts, but they would be severely tested by Juventus.

Close call during a classic against Juventus.

Paul and Mick Jones pressurise Piloni and Salvadore during a Leeds attack.

Crucial away goal … Paul (out of shot) watches his deflected shot wrong-foot Piloni for Leeds' opening goal.

Leeds United v. Juventus, 1971 Fairs Cup final second leg:

LEEDS UNITED: Sprake, Reaney, Cooper, Bremner (captain), Charlton, Hunter, Lorimer, Clarke, Jones, Giles, Madeley (Bates)

JUVENTUS: Tancredi, Spinosi, Marchetti, Furino, Morino, Salvadore, Haller, Causio, Anastasi, Capello, Bettaga

Allan gave us an early lead, but they soon equalised. Unfortunately, I sustained a nasty head injury so missed most of the game. I saw the remainder of the game from the stands and thought we defended well to clinch the trophy on away-goals.

The team was building towards its peak and we now had a tremendous balance throughout the side. The defence and midfield had been strong for some years, but Allan and Mick in attack complimented each other so well. Allan would pick up loose balls in an instant, whereas Mick played the target role to perfection. As a partnership they were the best I played

Ninety minutes from glory.

Piloni just gets to the ball first in the second-leg clash at Elland Road.

Paul's final is over following a nasty clash.

Celebration time after their Fairs Cup triumph.

with, and you have to give credit to Don for putting them together. They became renowned throughout Europe as the best around. How they never partnered England together was always a mystery to me. Playing international football, it took time to get used to new colleagues. Because of their understanding, I'm sure they would have been just as successful on the international front as at club level for Leeds.

Despite the disappointment in the League it was great to have won in Europe again, and on a personal level winning a first England cap had made my season.

Chapter Eight

THE HOLY GRAIL

1971/72

The big talking point throughout the close season centred around the Football Association's decision to ban Leeds from playing their opening four home games at Elland Road, following the pitch invasion in the infamous clash against West Brom. The club felt hard done by, and received mass media sympathy, but it did not stop the club receiving a heavy punishment from English football's governing body.

Pre-season Paul looked ahead to the new season in *Goal* magazine. Described by Ray Bradley as 'pound for pound' the most valuable professional in the First Division, Bradley was struck by the player's candid honesty as he reflected on his versatility, the 1974 World Cup and his priorities for the season. Paul told the reporter:

I've been a pro eight years now, but only a regular for three. I've learned to be patient and not been out of the side for the past two seasons now except for injuries, so being adaptable has obviously proved an asset in my case. Although as a professional I'm always prepared to play where I'm picked, I personally prefer to play in midfield because in addition to being in the game more you have a freer role. But I'll play for Leeds anywhere they want me. That's the way we've been brought up at Elland Road ... 'all for one and one for all'.

Regarding the next World Cup, I enjoy playing for England, but I honestly never worry about being picked. If I were lucky enough to be selected for the original 40 I'd be really eager to go. But if it means building myself up again at the last moment as in 1970 then I must honestly say no. There's more to life than just playing football. You've got to put these things in perspective without letting your personal and private life overlap. As for this season, I would really like to see Leeds win the FA Cup. Winning the cup is personally my biggest ambition.

Up against it from the start, Leeds started the season poorly, losing as many League games by mid-November as in the whole of the previous campaign. The opening three months of the season had seen them crash out of both the UEFA Cup, to Norwegian minnows Lierse SK, and the League Cup to West Ham.

Playing on a neutral ground did affect us. Although we stayed undefeated we dropped valuable points in two games. Our best performance in these 'home' matches was against Newcastle United when we won 5-1. I grabbed our fifth goal, before scoring our first a few days later in a 2-0 win against Crystal Palace. Needless to say we were glad to get back to Elland Road.

Above: Leeds United, 1971/72. From left to right, back row: Belfitt, Hunter, Sprake, Harvey, Jordan, Yorath. Middle row: Faulkner, Galvin, Jones, Madeley, Clarke, Charlton. Front row: Reaney, Bates, Lorimer, Giles, Bremner (captain), Davey, Cooper.

Left: Belgium blues!

Another Madeley goal, this time against Crystal Palace at Leeds' 'home' venue Leeds Road, Huddersfield.

The first game back was against Liverpool. The atmosphere was electric; we won 1-0 thanks to a Peter Lorimer strike.

During October there was a brief distraction for Paul with England playing a vital European Nations Cup tie. Despite having only gained one full cap at right-back, Paul was handed the key midfield task of marking Switzerland's play-maker Karl Odermatt.

Switzerland v. England, Nations Cup qualifying round

ENGLAND: Banks (Stoke City), Lawler (Liverpool), Cooper (Leeds United), Mullery (Tottenham Hotspur), McFarland (Derby County), Moore (West Ham, captain), Lee (Manchester City), Madeley (Leeds United), Chivers (Tottenham Hotspur), Hurst (West Ham), Peters (Tottenham Hotspur)

When I looked at the 16-man squad in the first place I thought there were nine certainties, which left a 7/2 chance for me. We won 3-2, which was a good result and I was pleased with my performance.

Four weeks later, England faced Switzerland in the return fixture, before completing their qualification campaign in Greece.

I played right-back against the Swiss; my first England match at Wembley. The atmosphere was fantastic. We were disappointed to only draw 1-1, which put pressure on our last game in Greece. Representing England at Wembley as opposed to Leeds was very different because the crowd was all on your side, but they expected you to perform or soon let you know. We won quite comfortably against Greece 2-0 to reach the knockout stages, which was pleasing. I was delighted to have broken into the team and was hopeful that I'd keep my place in the side.

England's workmanlike victory put them in the quarter-finals alongside Russia, West Germany, Italy, Belgium, Rumania, Hungary and Yugoslavia. When the draw was made it could have been kinder to England, who drew the tournament favourites West Germany. The tie was eagerly awaited and would give England an opportunity to avenge their World Cup quarter-final defeat in Mexico, though the Germans in turn had a score to settle as the last time they had played at Wembley was in the 1966 World Cup final.

Domestically, the opening third of the season had been blighted by injuries. In addition to Allan Clarke and Mick Jones struggling with knocks, Eddie Gray's absence meant Paul played the anchor role in midfield. Gray's return saw Paul switch

---

Headquarters in London:
GREAT WESTERN ROYAL HOTEL,
PADDINGTON, LONDON, W.2.
(Telephone: 01-723-8064)

Headquarters in Basle:
HOTEL ASCOT,
BASELSTRASSE 67—BACHTELENWEG 3,
4125 RIEHEN
(Telephone: 061 513951)

———

ARRANGEMENTS FOR TRAVEL
AND ACCOMMODATION

———

SUNDAY, 10th OCTOBER, 1971

ASSEMBLY. All players should make their own arrangements in order to arrive at the Great Western Royal Hotel, Paddington, London, W.2, by 20.00 hours.

MONDAY, 11th OCTOBER, 1971

10.00 hrs. Depart from Great Western Royal Hotel by motor coach for the Bank of England Sports Ground, Roehampton, where a training session will be held.

13.00 hrs. Lunch at Roehampton.

15.45 hrs. Depart from Bank of England Sports Ground, Roehampton, by motor coach for London Airport. (Terminal 1).

17.40 hrs. Depart from London Airport on Flight BE 792.

19.05 hrs. Arrive at Basle Airport. A motor coach will meet the party and convey them to the Hotel Ascot, which will be the Headquarters of the party during their stay in Basle.

TUESDAY, 12th OCTOBER, 1971

Arrangements for the morning will be announced at Headquarters.

15.00 hrs. Training Session at the Sankt Jacob Stadium.

20.00 hrs. Dinner for officials as guests of the Swiss Football Association.

WEDNESDAY, 13th OCTOBER, 1971

10.30 hrs. Training session at the F.C. Riehen Stadium.

Arrangements for the remainder of the day will be announced at Headquarters.

18.30 hrs. Depart from Hotel Ascot by motor coach for the Sankt Jacob Stadium.

20.00 hrs. SWITZERLAND v. ENGLAND.

22.15 hrs. Officials and players are invited to be the guests of the Swiss Football Association at an after-match reception.

THURSDAY, 14th OCTOBER, 1971

06.45 hrs. Depart from Hotel Ascot by motor coach for Basle Airport.

08.10 hrs. Depart from Basle Airport on Flight SR 820.

09.35 hrs. Arrive at London Airport (Terminal 2). A motor coach will meet the party and convey them to Lancaster Gate and main line railway stations.

Not much time for sightseeing on this England trip to Switzerland.

Leicester's Peter Shilton clears this attack, but was unable to stop Leeds winning 2-1.

to right-back following an injury to Paul Reaney. As players returned, Leeds redis-covered their form. Consecutive wins over Manchester City, Everton, Manchester United and Leicester City was part of a winning sequence of seven wins in eight games, as Leeds climbed the table rapidly.

Following a 2-0 win at Nottingham Forest, manager Matt Gillies told the *Express* that Leeds United were firing on all cylinders again. 'Make no mistake, Leeds are still the finest team in the country. They may have had their troubles early in the season but they are now showing real poise and assurance. They'll take some stopping.'

By Christmas a fine run of form saw Leeds back in the hunt for honours again. Just five points adrift from the top, a tremendous 2-0 win at Anfield on New Years Day put them back in the pack. The victory at Liverpool – the Anfield club's first home defeat in 35 matches, was a major turning point in the season. The team's form was impressive.

Alan Thompson, *Daily Express*: 'Leeds won magnificently. They have everything – ability, craft, flair, the ruthless streak, organisation and planning... Paul Madeley, everything that man does is economical of movement but successful in outcome.'

Barry Foster, *Yorkshire Post*: 'Leeds United are playing their most accomplished football since they became a major power in the game. Seldom has a team started the New Year so right on the field.'

We were reaching our peak. Despite the handicap of playing a number of matches on neutral grounds, which affected our results, we were back in the title race by the turn of the year and began to turn on the style.

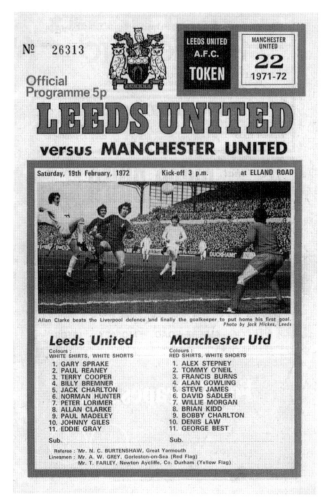

Nº 26313

LEEDS UNITED A.F.C.
TOKEN

MANCHESTER UNITED
22
1971-72

Official Programme 5p

LEEDS UNITED
versus **MANCHESTER UNITED**

Saturday, 19th February, 1972   Kick-off 3 p.m.   at ELLAND ROAD

Allan Clarke beats the Liverpool defence and finally the goalkeeper to put home his first goal.
Photo by Jock Hickes, Leeds

Leeds United
Colours :
WHITE SHIRTS, WHITE SHORTS
1. GARY SPRAKE
2. PAUL REANEY
3. TERRY COOPER
4. BILLY BREMNER
5. JACK CHARLTON
6. NORMAN HUNTER
7. PETER LORIMER
8. ALLAN CLARKE
9. PAUL MADELEY
10. JOHNNY GILES
11. EDDIE GRAY
Sub.

Manchester Utd
Colours :
RED SHIRTS, WHITE SHORTS
1. ALEX STEPNEY
2. TOMMY O'NEIL
3. FRANCIS BURNS
4. ALAN GOWLING
5. STEVE JAMES
6. DAVID SADLER
7. WILLIE MORGAN
8. BRIAN KIDD
9. BOBBY CHARLTON
10. DENIS LAW
11. GEORGE BEST
Sub.

Referee : Mr. N. C. BURTENSHAW, Great Yarmouth
Linesmen : Mr. A. W. GREY, Gorleston-on-Sea (Red Flag)
Mr. T. FARLEY, Newton Aycliffe, Co. Durham (Yellow Flag)

It doesn't get much better ... 5-1!

The coming weeks would see Leeds destroy Manchester United 5-1 and Southampton 7-0. The same Leeds XI played in both games: Sprake, Madeley, Cooper, Bremner (captain), Charlton, Hunter, Lorimer, Clarke, Jones, Giles, Gray.

Leeds' stunning win over their Pennine rivals produced rave reviews.

Brian Glanville, *Sunday Times*: 'The spectacle was almost that of the matador toying with a weary bull, the delighted roars of the crowd at each new piece of virtuosity the equivalent of the 'oles' of the bullring.'

Ronald Crowther, *Daily Mail*: 'Leeds, as we saw in this superb display of selfless, non-stop running, are essentially a team without any exhibitionist or would-be virtuoso. They had eleven stars all clinically efficient in this demolition of their arch-rivals from Manchester.'

Tom Holley, *Yorkshire Evening Post*: 'Rampant Leeds completed their 'double double' over the Manchester clubs, and if you think the Old Trafford men were 'tanned' you are dead right. It should have been 10-1.'

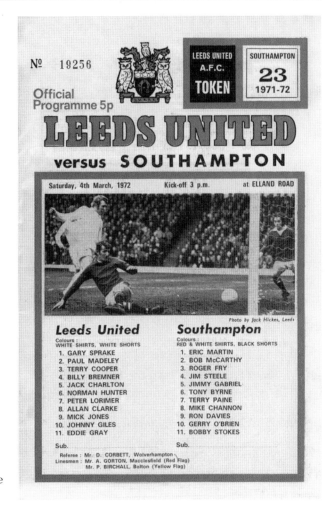

Ole! Ole! ... Saints are slaughtered 7-0.

Leeds' display against Southampton made neutrals gasp on *Match of the Day's* televised coverage, their sustained game of keep ball when the match was comprehensively won, as much as the quality of football winning acclaim.

After the match an ecstatic Don Revie told reporters, 'Compassion it might have been, contempt it certainly was not. Theirs is the glory. They have said it all for me. I'm not saying anything. I've said it all before. You say it'.

They did ...

Michael Worth, *Sunday Express*: 'Remember the scoreline! It marked the day Leeds United unveiled a treasure trove of memorable football riches ... If it all seemed too easy, it was only because superb Leeds, made it look that way. Southampton belonged to another league; Leeds to another world'.

Mike Casey, *Yorkshire Evening Post*: 'Skill, individual flair, teamwork, non-stop effort and devastating marksmanship ... Don Revie's Championship claimants had all these virtues in abundance'.

Michael Carey: 'Southampton were reduced to a cheap replica of a First Division side by a display of sustained, often breathtaking brilliance. Slaughter of the not-so-innocents, one might say. If it had been a boxing match or a horse race there would have been a stewards' inquiry into Southampton's limp performance. Many a towel had been thrown in before the end.'

Saints defender Jimmy Gabriel: 'Leeds have just about reached perfection … They are the nearest thing to footballing utopia. They used to be hard, niggling and unpopular, but they've come through all the phases and developed into a truly wonderful side. They're telepathic. You don't hear their players shout, they seem to know just where their mates are. Leeds have now reached the stage where they could destroy any side.'

Southampton manager, Ted Bates: 'When you see a team play like they did you must rate them as one of the finest in the world.'

Everyone recalls the Manchester United and Southampton clashes in front of the Match of the Day *cameras, but we also thumped Nottingham Forest 6-1. Manchester may not have been the force they used to be, but we destroyed them in the second half. As for Southampton, after going seven up we began playing 'keep-ball' towards the end. I remember Allan, Billy and John flicking the ball about, someone had to lose the ball, which happened to be me, but I quickly won it back because I knew the stick I'd get after if I didn't! We played some magnificent football and scored some great goals, although at times it was a shade cavalier. I had to cover all over the pitch with everybody wanting to get in on the scoring. What summed up our superiority for me was when I played a ball to Norman who ran around the left flank and crossed for Big Jack to nod home. Our two centre-halves combining in attack from open play … it was just incredible. I'd never known a performance like it!*

The team received national acclaim, a point acknowledged by Don Revie in an interview with John Sadler.

When we came into the First Division eight years ago they slung a terrible cruel tag around our necks. They called us the dirtiest team in the land; that was a lousy label to give a team of youngsters. We were booed on every ground, booked for almost every hard tackle. It's only now that we've managed to live it down. Now they are accepting us as a great team. I would like the current team to be remembered as ambassadors of football. I'm sure in years to come they will talk about us as one of the truly great football sides of world football. We are reaching the stage where we don't need to be compared to anyone. We are who we are – Leeds United. We've learned to have absolute belief in our ability. We believe in ourselves and at last other people seem to believe in us.

Apart from being back in the title race, Leeds were through to the semi-finals of the FA Cup.

Every season we were determined to have a go at the cup, and after the embarrassment of losing to Colchester we were even more determined when we met lower division clubs. I remember Don Revie saying before the Bristol Rovers game let's set our stall out from the kick off.

Leeds cup run began with an opening round 4-1 win over Bristol Rovers before the fourth-round draw took them to Liverpool at Anfield for the tie of the round.

It was a really tough battle but we held out for a deserved replay after drawing 0-0.

Following the 'backs-to-the-wall' display Eric Todd of the *Guardian* pondered the definition of a 'typical' cup tie. 'If it may be interpreted as meaning skill, hard tacking, near misses, over eagerness, carelessness and a refusal to surrender, then Anfield witnessed such a game'.

Two goals from 'Sniffer' Clarke in the replay, played on a Wednesday afternoon due to the miner's strike, brought Leeds a fifth-round clash at Cardiff City. Following the game, referee Gordon Hill applauded the players off the pitch. Hill said, 'It was my way of saying thank-you to both teams for two wonderful games.' Alan Thompson, *Daily Express*, was also impressed: 'It was the type of match between two titanic sides who could have thrilled the crowd for hours. Allan Clarke snuffed out Liverpool's FA Cup hopes with a couple of goals that only the likes of he would the audacity to attempt.'

After brushing aside Cardiff City, the match settled by a John Giles brace, Leeds were firm favourites for the cup.

Michael Boon of the *Sunday Express* commented: 'Smooth as cream … Leeds are as rich in talent as any club side in the world.'

On the train journey back to Leeds we heard the quarter-final draw on the radio. Just as we were approaching a tunnel there were two balls left Tottenham and ourselves. We were delighted to get the home draw, because they were something of a bogey side to us. Apart from doing the 'double' the previous season; they had also beaten us a few weeks before.

For the Tottenham clash razzmatazz came to town!

Tottenham were a good side and had some fine players in their side, with the likes of Pat Jennings, Mike England, Martin Peters and Alan Gilzean. In attack they had Martin Chivers who was a real handful and a really strong player. Norman used to give him stick when he marked him. He also gave me stick when I had to mark him, because my style of tackling was never as robust! Martin was always a handful to mark but always polite. Norman would say, 'after you Martin' … he'd reply 'no after you squire'. It was all good harmless banter.

The atmosphere throughout the game was electric, one of the best games I ever played in at Elland Road. For this match we wore stocking tabs for the first time, which our supporters loved. We also had personalised tracksuits, and warmed up before the game with a set routine.

Les Cocker would impersonate a sergeant major, whilst in pairs we'd be hopping and skipping to loosen up. It was no more than how we warmed up on a training pitch, but supporters had never seen anything like it before. The atmosphere built into a frenzy. Of course the occasion was heightened because it was a quarter-final clash, a packed house and two big teams were involved. Nowadays the warm up is the norm, but in 1972 it was very different, and we did it everywhere we went afterwards.

Tottenham took the lead through a long-range cross that Gary misjudged. Many teams would have been despondent conceding a goal like that, but Billy urged us forward demanding an immediate response. Billy was everything people thought, tenacious, good on the ball, and he had a great attitude. His main strength as captain was his ability to motivate and he was always encouraging during a game. This was one of those occasions and Allan equalised just before the half-time interval, before Big Jack headed the winner for a hard-fought sucess. However, we should have won far more comfortably but Pat Jennings was in inspired form and made a stack of world-class saves.

The media had a field day with Leeds performance.

Brian James, *Sunday Times*: 'As many moments of near perfection as football can get.'

Eric Todd, *Guardian*: 'On this form, Leeds are irresistible. They have some outstanding individuals, Madeley alone is worth £300,000 of anybody's money, and when those individuals put the team before self-aggrandisement and pool their assets, the result is awesome.'

Hugh McIlvanney, *Observer*: 'Only bigots can now bet against them (Leeds) in the competition. This was a day when comparisons with the greatest of European teams could not be dismissed as ludicrous arrogance. Their football was breathtaking in its scope and fluency, alive with dazzling improvisations. The full intimidating depth of their quality has never been more manifest than it was in those early minutes. There was scarcely a weakness to be seen and excellence everywhere'.

Terry Brindle, *Yorkshire Post*: 'Leeds should be a short-price for the Boat Race, the Grand National and the British Grand Prix, let alone the Cup!'

Don Warters, *Yorkshire Evening Post*: 'The twin towers of Wembley are beckoning and Leeds United are answering them loud and clear.'

Don Revie, was ecstatic: 'In the first 20 minutes we saw absolute soccer perfection'. Tottenham manager Bill Nicholson said: 'My players thought they could play until they saw this. Leeds were unforgettable.' Pat Jennings who made numerous world-class saves to keep the score respectable said Leeds were the best club he had ever faced. He added: 'They might as well give Leeds the FA Cup now. I can't see any team left in the competition that could beat them on the form they have been showing over the last few weeks.'

Safely through to the semi-finals, Leeds returned to the title race alongside Manchester City, Liverpool and Derby County. Following a costly defeat at Derby's notorious Baseball Ground, Leeds bounced back with victories over Huddersfield Town and Stoke City, but at a heavy price, because Terry Cooper broke a leg at the Victoria Ground just a week before Leeds' FA Cup semi-final clash with Birmingham City.

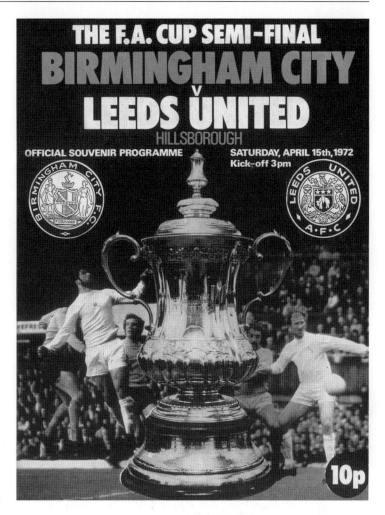

Next stop Wembley.

The cup run had once again demonstrated Paul's versatility. Beginning at centre-half due to an injury to Jack Charlton for the opening two games, Paul deputised for Mick Jones (a late withdrawal) in the Liverpool replay. During the game an injury to Paul Reaney saw a switch to right-back where he would stay through the fifth round and quarter-final matches. Terry Cooper's injury meant transferring to left-back for the semi-final. Four positional changes – something few footballers could achieve seamlessly.

Only Birmingham City now stood in Leeds' way of a third FA Cup final, and Leeds strode effortlessly to a 3-0 win to book a place in the Centenary FA Cup final, where they would face Arsenal. Leeds' victory had been clinical.

James Mossop, *Sunday Express*: 'Don Revie's masters turned on a show that was something special: a strolling show of style, grace and skill that brought rare moments of soccer magic. Not for Leeds the nervous, frenzied play that traditionally reduces semi-finals to scrappy, scrambling affairs.'

Eric Todd, *Guardian*: 'Only once on Saturday did Birmingham City take the Mickey out of Leeds United, and because it happened before the game it didn't really matter.'

Brian James, *Sunday Times*: 'A result as inevitable as tomorrow's dawn'.

Before the semi-final at Hillsborough, Birmingham came out early and did their warm up around the centre circle, mimicking us. Maybe Freddie Goodwin was trying to out-fox us, but it failed to work because it was over by half-time after Mick and Peter scored, and we ran out comfortable winners. The match though was also notable for David Harvey being chosen as first choice 'keeper in preference to Gary Sprake. Over the years Gary had been a fine goal-keeper, and could be inspirational, but his occasional blunders had proved costly. Don had clearly decided it was time for a change, David was a steady 'keeper and had never let the team down when he played. The timing was unusual, with it being such a big game, but it was the right decision. David finally received his break and took it.

Overcoming Birmingham was great, but there was no great celebration, we wanted to finish the job. After the Chelsea defeat Don said we'd be back; he was right. My most poignant memory of the dressing room scenes afterwards was Terry Cooper hobbling over towards me. Despite his own personal disappointment at missing out on Wembley he was absolutely thrilled for everybody.

The popular weekly
magazine's Cup Final special.

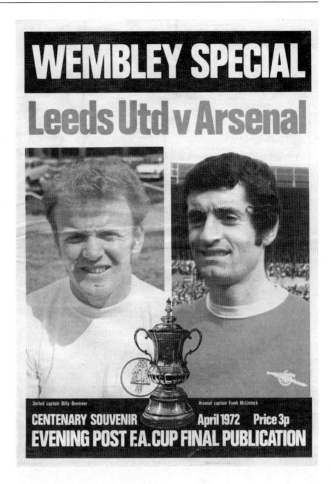

WEMBLEY SPECIAL
Leeds Utd v Arsenal

United captain Billy Bremner · Arsenal captain Frank McLintock

CENTENARY SOUVENIR · April 1972 · Price 3p
EVENING POST F.A. CUP FINAL PUBLICATION

Yorkshire Evening Post FA Cup
final special.

Following their routine victory, Leeds slipped up at Newcastle before recording wins
over West Brom and Chelsea. One League game remained, at Wolves, but the FA
ruled it would have to take place just forty-eight hours after the Cup Final against
Arsenal. With only three weeks between the semi-final and final, the build up was
hectic. The players were fitted with their Wembley suits and recorded the traditional
Cup Final song.

Numerous articles were also published. *Goal* magazine produced a 'Wembley
Ratings' chart for each of the finalist players. Their ratings for Paul read: 'Ball skill 8,
passing 8, defensive ability 9, attacking ability 8, temperament 10. Judgement: His
versatility, strength, unselfishness and ability make him one of the outstanding footballers in the country. Wherever he plays he'll do a great job.'

As for the club's 'Official Wembley Special', it gave a brief profile on each player.
Amongst a host of 'useful' information, fans were informed that Paul's most embar-
rassing moment was being constantly mistaken for Alan Peacock when he was
virtually unknown. Personal likes were shredded wheat and poached egg on toast for
breakfast, whilst his biggest superstition was having a liking to walk under ladders!

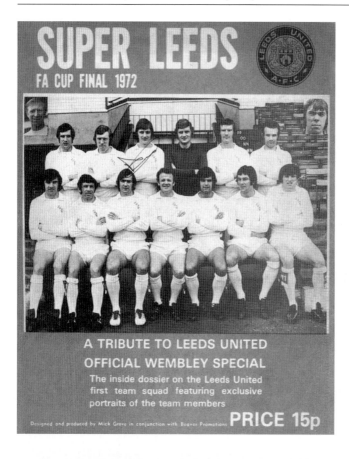

Leeds United's official commemorative brochure.

Pop Idols!

Paul's dad and Ann's mum tie the knot.

It was amusing seeing all the articles written and memorabilia brought out for the Cup Final. Some were unusual to say the least! Our record 'Leeds Leeds Leeds' is not exactly a musical classic, however it's still popular with supporters today, but is better known as 'Marching on Together'. We went to recording studios near Manchester to record the song; it was a real laugh. There were some horrible voices amongst the players, so the producers put in a couple of 'ringers' to boost the vocals! In addition, during our final preparations, my father married Ann's mother three days before the final. It was certainly a tight schedule.

We couldn't wait for the final. We knew it would be tight against Arsenal but after losing out to Chelsea in 1970 we were determined not to slip up again. At the back of our minds we knew the 'double' was only two matches away, but as the old cliché goes we just took one game at a time.

Our build-up followed the normal pattern, even though there were more Press than for a normal game. We played bingo and carpet bowls before watching a video of the Southampton win. Don's great friend Herbert Warner was helping to relax us with jokes and calling out the bingo numbers. We had our pre-match team-talk when Don went through his 'dossier'. The team was confident, relaxed and ready.

Match day, there was the extra buzz that only a cup final can generate. After our pre-match meal we watched 'Cup Final' Grandstand before Don's main team-talk. Before long we began our journey to Wembley. The scenes turning into Wembley Way was fantastic. Shortly after arriving we took a look at the pitch. The conditions could not have contrasted more favourably than my previous Cup Final; it was hot and the pitch was perfect.

After changing, Don gave us his final instructions, and then it was time to line up in the tunnel. Waiting was the worst part, you just wanted to get out, but the adrenaline rush as you walk out was incredible. It's part of the day, whether you win, lose or draw to experience going out there as a player is something really special. I was lucky to play there a number of times and loved the unique atmosphere generated by making the long walk up the tunnel and onto the famous pitch.

The noise from the crowd when we emerged was incredible. I was sixth out after Norman and my stomach was going like hell; I just wanted to get on with it. I've often joked that it was nearly bad enough to turn round and go back in again! Because it was the competition's centenary we walked out between a special pageant in celebration. After the introductions we were soon kicking the ball about before kick off. The nerves seemed to just drain away as I concentrated on the game.

Arsenal v. Leeds United, 1972 FA Cup final:

ARSENAL: Barnett, Rice, McNab, Storey, McLintock (captain), Simpson, Armstrong, Ball, Radford (Kennedy), Graham, George

LEEDS UNITED: Harvey, Reaney, Madeley, Bremner (captain), Charlton, Hunter, Lorimer, Clarke, Jones, Giles, Gray

In the first half both sides had opportunities. Paul cleared off the line from an Alan Ball shot and David saved comfortably from a Frank McLintock snap shot. For us Mick shaved a post and Allan went close with a couple of efforts. We were relaxed at the interval and felt in control.

Eight minutes into the second half Leeds made the breakthrough with a classic header from Allan Clarke. The move began when Jack Charlton broke up an Arsenal attack led by Ball, before passing to Paul, who brought the ball out of defence. Feeding Peter Lorimer, the Scot in turn found Mick Jones free on the edge of the penalty area. Out-muscling Bob McNab, Jones rode the left-back's challenge to flight a centre into the penalty area. Clarke launched himself to head the ball beyond the despairing dive of Geoff Barnett into the Arsenal net.

It wasn't a classic final but throughout we were fairly solid. We didn't play to the same level as against Chelsea in 1970 when we turned them inside out, but we were worthy winners. Allan scored a cracking goal, which I had a minor role in and we only had a couple of anxious moments late on, especially when Charlie George hit the cross bar. The last ten minutes just seemed to take an age. On hearing the final whistle I remember hugging David and Norman. Collecting the medal and lap of honour was fantastic, though they were over far too quickly.

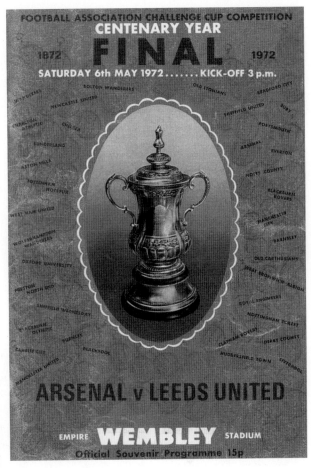

Above: Destiny awaits.

Left: Will the number 3 stocking tag be lucky for Paul.

Bertie Mee and Don Revie lead their teams out before the centenary cup final.

The Duke of Edinburgh meets Billy and his troops.

THE SPORTSMAN'S WORLD OF

Soccer

Edited by Martin Tyler

We've won the cup ... Paul, David Harvey and Norman Hunter celebrate at the final whistle.

My overriding feeling was one of relief that we had finally won the FA Cup. Having lost two previous finals, there was added pressure going into this one because we did not want to be remembered as the team that always lost cup finals. In the dressing room after I remember Terry coming in, he'd been doing a bit of television work. I gave him one of my stocking tags as my personal memento. Unfortunately there was no time to really savour the moment as we had go straight to Wolverhampton after the match to try and clinch the 'double'.

The best team had won.

Alan Hoby, *Sunday Express*: 'The elegant stylists of Leeds have won the FA Cup for the first time. Whatever happens, the beaten finalists of 1965 and 1970 have at last killed the sneer that they always stumble at the final hurdle. That taunt lies buried forever beneath the damp green turf of Wembley.'

Hugh McIlvanney, *Observer*: 'Don Revie's Leeds United, the team who had come to regard Wembley as a place of near misses, won the FA Cup at their third attempt yesterday, when they outplayed Arsenal to an extent that was inadequately reflected in the scoreline. It was Leeds whose football was more controlled, whose ideas the

At last!

more inventive. Once Leeds had settled, and especially after their goal, they dominated Arsenal confidently.'

Frank Butler, *News of the World*: 'Leeds well deserved their victory after they got out of the Yale-lock grip of the Arsenal defensive system in the first half. A goal was needed to break the Arsenal system and what a great goal Leeds scored. Leeds had always looked the more classy footballing side. Once they scored they blossomed out like superman. Suddenly Arsenal looked tired, beaten and very ordinary.'

David Miller, *Sunday Telegraph*: 'Leeds, the most consistent team in European soccer for the last eight years, carried off the centenary FA Cup in a final which was eventually one-sided. From the start Leeds were transparently the better side and by the finish they had outplayed the opposition in almost every phase of the game, even if they only controlled it for that last half-hour.'

Frank McGhee, *Sunday Mirror*: 'Arsenal could have tried for another 100 years and still would not have a serious chance of beating Leeds. Not on the form, the mood and the manpower seen in this centenary cup final.'

Albert Barham, *Guardian*: 'A new name, Leeds United will be inscribed on the plinth of the FA Cup this centenary year and few will deny that the honour has been long overdue. A spectacularly headed goal by Clarke was insufficient reward for the superiority of Leeds in every department of the game. They could and should have had a couple more afterwards.'

GREEN POST

SATURDAY MAY 6 1972   No. 26,984   Tel: LEEDS 32701   Price 3p

Leeds United supporters with plenty to shout about in Trafalgar Square.

IT'S YOURS, UNITED

£5,000 and car in Pick the Spot

Pages 2 and 9

Free transfer for cup hero and Storrie

FRANCIS ACCEPTS

SCOTTISH CUP FINAL

RESULT: Gls.
CELTIC 6
HIBERNIAN 1

Geoff Barnett, Arsenal goalkeeper, saves from Mick Jones, Leeds United centre-forward, in the air at Wembley. The United players on the left are Peter Lorimer and Allan Clarke.

Reaney 'rescue act' yet again

By MIKE CASEY

Conteh sprints to hat-trick

Death ends family Cup Final plan

Clarke header brings Cup to Elland Road: 1-0

CUP WINNERS AT LAST! LEEDS UNITED WON THE F.A. CUP CENTENARY FINAL AGAINST ARSENAL AT WEMBLEY BY 1-0.

Allan Clarke headed the vital goal from Mick Jones's precision pass after 53 minutes. There were four bookings—McNab and George (Arsenal), Hunter and Bremner (Leeds).

By DON WARTERS

GRAY'S CHASE

GANTON TURF

SHREWD PASS

CLARKE FELLED

GRAY GROUNDED

ENCOURAGED

ACROSS GOAL

David Harvey, Leeds goalkeeper, safely gathers the ball in the Cup Final. In close attendance are Charlie George, Arsenal centre-forward, and Norman Hunter, Leeds United left-back.

United had a lot off to the 39th minute, when a quick lead-up by Arsenal led to Ball having a shot blocked.

Cricket scores

LEAGUE CUP

CAMBRIDGE UNIV. v. WORCESTER

GLOUCESTER v. HAMPSHIRE

KENT v. SUSSEX

LANCASHIRE v. DERBY

NORTHANTS v. WARWICK

RESULT: Gls.
LEEDS UNITED 1
ARSENAL 0

MINOR COUNTIES (N.)

SURREY v. ESSEX

MINOR COUNTIES (S.) v. GLAMORGAN

Aussie Soccer Results

The *Green Post* reports on Leeds' victory.

Terry Brindle, *Yorkshire Post*: 'It was the day on which Leeds United proved beyond question that they are a great side. A day on which the most coveted trophy in soccer was added to their impressive pedigree, and no side which has not won the cup can claim to true greatness.'

Tragically, the win had come at a price because Mick was injured in the last minute, which meant he would miss our crucial League match at Wolves.

On a night of unbearable tension, Leeds battled away despite the handicap of playing Clarke, Giles and Gray with injuries that would normally have seen them rested, and but for poor refereeing would have clinched the Championship and 'double'. Two-down early in the second half, Bremner gave Leeds hope when he converted Madeley's diagonal cross, and almost snatched a draw and the title in the last minute, but his backward header was cleared off the line. Heartbreakingly, Leeds had been denied a deserved 'double'.

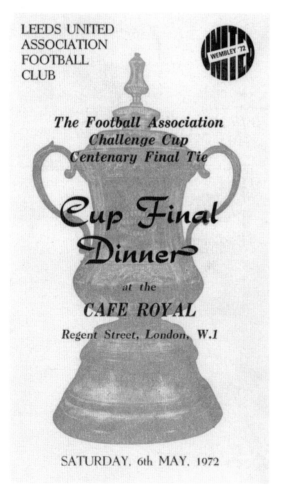

LEEDS UNITED
ASSOCIATION
FOOTBALL
CLUB

WEMBLEY '72

The Football Association
Challenge Cup
Centenary Final Tie

Cup Final
Dinner

at the

CAFE ROYAL

Regent Street, London, W.1

SATURDAY, 6th MAY, 1972

Celebration time … but not for Revie and his troops as a crack at the 'double' awaits at Wolves.

It's not to be ... the 'double' dream dies at Molineux.

Alan Thompson, *Daily Express*: 'Leeds failed by 23 minutes to complete a magnificent 'double' ... but though the record books will never show it, they are for me the FA Cup winners and League Champions.'

Don Warters, *Yorkshire Evening Post*: 'If ever a team had cause to feel bitter, United have today. Leeds should have received three penalties. For the players it must have felt like knives being driven slowly into their backs.'

A bitterly disappointed Don Revie said, 'I thought we should have had three clear penalties. It was definitely hands twice. It's just too much. When you get decisions like that going against you, what can you do, but I was proud of the team even in defeat.'

It was incredible but again we were on the wrong side of some crucial decisions by the referee, and lost 2-1. It was hard to take, because I believe we deserved the title that term, having come back from the handicap of playing three games on neutral grounds. The dressing room was so quiet because we deserved to win a 'double' as a team, which at the time had only been achieved by three sides.

Despite the heartbreak, Leeds had at last won the FA Cup ...

There's something very special about Wembley on Cup Final day that effects even the hardest of professional footballers. You remember how you watched FA Cup finals as a kid, remember how it was always 'the' day of the football season, and it was a major ambition I'd set myself.

Leeds United, 1972 FA Cup winners. From left to right, back row: Reaney, Charlton, Harvey, Jones, Hunter, Madeley. Front row: Lorimer, Clarke, Bremner (captain), Giles, Bates, Gray.

When I was lucky enough to play in one and you hear that fantastic explosion of noise, and feel the butterflies as you walk out of the tunnel, you realise what people mean by 'Wembley magic'. I'd been close before, losing in two semi-finals and a final, so the centenary final is very special. It's a tournament that has such a rich history. I was brought up with it as a schoolboy, so winning at Wembley in 1972 was very special for me, and it's a day I'll never forget. The win against Arsenal is my favourite one-off playing memory.

On the international scene Paul played in both Nations Cup quarter-final clashes with West Germany, in addition to playing against Wales and Scotland in the Home International Championships.

West Germany won the first leg at Wembley 3-1, to take control of the tie, which we were unable to pull back in Berlin. Our 0-0 draw meant we were defeated on aggregate, which was very disappointing. I know they had the likes of Beckenbauer, Muller and Netzer in their side, but we were also pretty useful. I recall the second leg particularly, because straight after the Wolves match, Norman and I were whisked off to prepare for the match in Berlin. The pair of us never saw the light of day! Despite the huge disappointment of losing to West Germany, on a personal level I'd played in seven of the internationals during the season. With the World Cup qualifying campaign about to begin I was delighted that I would play a part.

Chapter Nine

DOUBLE CUP DISASTER

1972/73

Pre-season Leeds were one of the bookies' favourites for honours again. Despite an opening day 4-0 defeat against Chelsea results soon picked up, even though performances failed to reach the heights of the previous season. Leeds' lack of consistency found the Press beginning to write them off, which was incredible considering the elite writers on Fleet Street had voted five Leeds players into the Rothmans top XI during the summer. The Golden Boots Awards, in its third year, was a prestigious honour for players. However, following a defeat at home to Liverpool, Eric Todd of the *Guardian* wrote: 'They must accept that Giles and Charlton are past their peak, and that Bremner's overworked batteries are running low ... Leeds have achieved many things but now ... the writing is on the wall.'

It was incredible the stories some journalists wrote at times. There was never a middle ground, you were either heroes or villains. It didn't affect us though, although we were aware what some journalists were writing. We'd been the most consistent side for years so we just let our results do the talking.

Ignoring their critics Leeds bounced back, hammering the defending champions Derby County 5-0 and one of the front-runners Everton 2-1. Following the win at Goodison, Norman Wynne wrote, 'laugh off any suggestion that Leeds are slipping. They dismissed Everton as a team of Championship hopefuls with a display of efficient football that was almost as colourful as their all-yellow strip.' The media was fickle!

Leeds embarked on a sixteen-match run, which would bring just a solitary defeat. Six more wins at the turn of the year put Leeds back among the pacemakers, however, there were worrying echoes of 1970 as Leeds made progress in the FA Cup and European Cup Winners Cup...

Playing his part was Paul. Derek Potter *Express* (2 December 1972) saluted the man of the season for him.

He lopes rather than chases. He glides into a tackle where others tear in. But the biggest give-away to his class is time. The time he always seems to have in reserve to stop an attack, contain or beat an opponent and leisurely stroke the ball forward. Paul Madeley is arguably Britain's most valuable player worth the

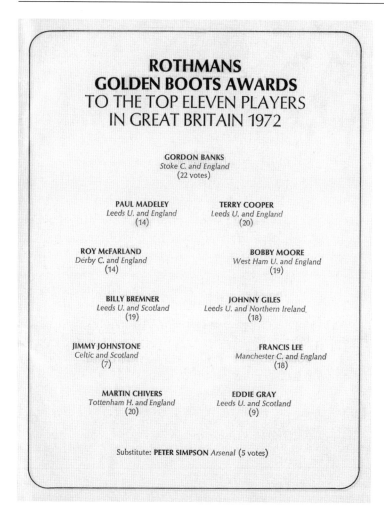

**ROTHMANS
GOLDEN BOOTS AWARDS
TO THE TOP ELEVEN PLAYERS
IN GREAT BRITAIN 1972**

GORDON BANKS
Stoke C. and England
(22 votes)

PAUL MADELEY
Leeds U. and England
(14)

TERRY COOPER
Leeds U. and England
(20)

ROY McFARLAND
Derby C. and England
(14)

BOBBY MOORE
West Ham U. and England
(19)

BILLY BREMNER
Leeds U. and Scotland
(19)

JOHNNY GILES
Leeds U. and Northern Ireland.
(18)

JIMMY JOHNSTONE
Celtic and Scotland
(7)

FRANCIS LEE
Manchester C. and England
(18)

MARTIN CHIVERS
Tottenham H. and England
(20)

EDDIE GRAY
Leeds U. and Scotland
(9)

Substitute: **PETER SIMPSON** *Arsenal* (5 votes)

Top team!

topside of £250,000 to any club. There is a touch of Bobby Moore in him and more than a touch of John Charles. He has an Adonis physique and the temperament to use it to the full advantage of himself and his team. Only two bookings in almost nine years is a tribute in itself. What other player can: play either flank in the back four, at centre-half, and operate in midfield or attack? He would play in goal if Don Revie asked him to, and he would play well!

The article entitled 'The Madeley Number Always Comes Up' included an analysis of the number of times he had worn each shirt for Leeds since making his debut on 11 January 1964. Playing 247 out of 372 League games, the shirt breakdown makes interesting reading. No 2 shirt – 42 games; No 3 – 39; No 4 – 10; No 5 – 31; No 6 – 3; No 7 – 9; No 8 – 36; No 9 – 18; No 10 – 9; No 11 – 50. Madeley has also adorned 53 European games plus many assorted home cup-ties and scored 29 goals in the process.

Above: Leeds United, 1972/73. From left to right, back row: Cherry, Madeley, Jones, Ellam, Jordan, Charlton. Middle row: Reaney, Galvin, Harvey, Sprake, Hunter, Clarke. Front row: Lorimer, Giles, Bremner (captain), Bates, Gray, Yorath.

Left: Another FA Cup run and West Brom struggle to cope with Mr Versatile and Sniffer during a 2-0 defeat.

As FA Cup holders, Leeds began their first European Cup Winners Cup campaign. Their first venue was the intimidating atmosphere of Ankara; but after gaining a draw against Ankaragucu, Leeds squeezed home 2-1 on aggregate before facing a tough encounter behind the Iron Curtain against the East German side Carl Zeiss Jena.

With years of experience behind them, nothing phased the players who ground out a creditable 0-0 draw before winning the home leg 2-0. The quarter-final against Rapid Bucharest however was far more comfortable, a 5-0 win in the home leg at Elland Road making the return a formality.

The clash against Rapid was one that I could not forget, because straight after the match I had to rush off to the maternity ward because Ann was just about to give birth to our second child. I only just made it … Nicholas arrived shortly after midnight on 8 March; it was some day!

Before the semi-final however, the team were putting the finishing touches to a fine FA Cup run. Beginning with a tricky tie against Norwich City, the Canaries proved tough opponents to crack. It took Leeds three games to make it through to the next round, a 5-0 win in the second replay settling matters. Following relatively comfortable wins against Plymouth Argyle and West Brom at Elland Road, Leeds were drawn to face Brian Clough's Derby County side in the quarter-finals at their notorious Baseball ground.

Playing at the Baseball Ground was always tough because the pitch was heavily sanded, which made it difficult to play flowing football. The atmosphere was similar to Upton Park (West Ham) and the Dell (Southampton) because the crowd was almost in the back of the net. At Stamford Bridge (Chelsea) however, I always felt it was a big advantage to the away team because the fans were such a distance from you. Of course though if you were winning at an away ground or losing at home the crowd noise was very noticeable!

Leeds warmed up for the cup clash with a 3-2 win in the League, and were determined to make it a double after Derby had pipped them to the title the previous season. In a fiercely contested match, Revie's team was indebted to a 'Hotshot' Lorimer special for their place in the semi-finals.

Barry Foster of the *Yorkshire Post* was impressed: 'Leeds were in an invincible mood, complete in every department. Once Peter Lorimer supplied the killer punch, Derby County might as well have put their clocks on there and then for British Summer Time and gone home.'

In the semi-finals Leeds faced Wolves at Maine Road, giving them an opportunity to avenge their League defeat at Molineux at the end of the previous season that had cost them the 'double'.

With Norman Hunter injured, I partnered Big Jack, but early on he suffered an injury forcing us to reshuffle with Terry Yorath moving back from midfield. Far from being weakened, we

Official Programme — **F.A. Cup Semi Final**

LEEDS UNITED
v
WOLVERHAMPTON WANDERERS

Ninety minutes from the 'Twin Towers'.

7th April 1973 at Maine Road, Manchester   10p

demonstrated our strength in depth and took control. Terry was a rock in defence and Billy scored the all-important winner late on. Incredibly, this was his third winner in FA Cup semi-finals to book our third trip to Wembley in four seasons. Awaiting us this time were outsiders Sunderland from the Second Division, who had surprisingly knocked out Manchester City and Arsenal. We were made hot favourites with the bookmakers.

Four days after the win over Wolves, Leeds attempted to reach their fourth European final against the crack Yugoslavian side Hajduk Split. The first leg, which Paul missed, was a tense affair. Leeds won with a goal from 'Sniffer' Clarke, who was later sent off after retaliating to a vicious challenge by a Split defender. The return was a tight encounter, but Leeds drew on all their years of experience to draw 0-0 and reach another European final. Their opponents would be Italian giants AC Milan.

Above: Job done ... bring on
Sunderland.

Right: I think we know the
way ...

It was a tremendous achievement reaching another final, but we knew we'd be missing key players with Billy and Allan suspended.

The team's achievement did not go unnoticed.

Derek Wallis, *Daily Mirror*: 'Leeds United can now claim to be arguably the greatest team that English football has known. Greater even than the phenomenal Arsenal team of the '30s, than Spurs of the early '60s, greater even than Manchester United of so many post-war years. Love them or hate them, and curiously there are still more ready to swear at them than by them, there can be no dispute that Leeds are the team of at least the last decade ... The greatest English club team ever? I wouldn't argue against it.'

With Leeds still going well in the League, a treble was once again within reach, but such talk soon disappeared as the effort in reaching the two finals caught up with the players. Just one win in their last six League games saw Leeds finish their League campaign in third place and the week before the FA Cup final, with their league challenge over; Revie played only Peter Lorimer from his first-team squad against Birmingham City as his side rested.

Going into the final, sports writers featured Paul because he would be wearing his sixth different shirt in a major cup final. This astonishing fact intrigued statisticians looking for a different angle on the game. His record read: League Cup final 1968 (number 9), Fairs Cup final 1968 (number 8), FA Cup 1970 (number 2), Fairs Cup 1971 (number 11), FA Cup 1972 (number 3). For the Sunderland clash he was due to play number 5, making him the most versatile cup finalist ever!

Leeds United v. Sunderland, FA Cup final:

LEEDS UNITED: Harvey, Reaney, Cherry, Bremner (captain), Madeley, Hunter, Lorimer, Clarke, Jones, Giles, Gray (Yorath)

SUNDERLAND: Montgomery, Malone, Guthrie, Horswill, Watson, Pitt; Kerr (captain), Hughes, Halom, Porterfield, Tueart

Leeds may have been overwhelming favourites but Sunderland upset the odds to win. Today their triumph is acknowledged as the greatest FA Cup final upset of all-time. To Leeds United's credit, everyone connected with the club, though naturally shattered, handled the 1–0 defeat graciously. Don Revie commented after the game: 'Give credit to Sunderland, they were full of enthusiasm and running. We are making no excuses.' Disappointed and defiant, Revie added, 'We'll be back again; we start in July.'

For Derek Wallis of the *Daily Mirror*, the FA Cup would never be the same again. 'The harsh, fiercely competitive world of football, which breeds giants sparingly and their conquerors occasionally, is still in a state of shock following the most sensational FA Cup result of all time. If a Second Division team of limited experience can beat a First Division opposition of such stature at Wembley there are no giants left to be killed anywhere else.'

Above: Paul's third FA Cup final in four years.

Right: Here we go ...

Paul goes close early on before Sunderland strike and Montgomery makes his wonder save.

We underperformed on the day against Sunderland, although you have to give them credit; they worked hard. We had a full team out apart from Jack, who was injured and retired at the end of the season. Some people say a team's name is on the cup, and after Jim Montgomery's miraculous save from Peter, maybe they were destined to win it. Of course you keep trying, but when you miss a gilt-edged chance it does knock confidence. Naturally, all the papers knocked us and said we were finished, but we knew that we weren't. Many pundits forgot that Sunderland had defeated Manchester City in the quarter-finals and Arsenal in the semis so they were no mugs and had some good players coming through like Dave Watson and Denis Tueart. However, there were no excuses, we let ourselves down and didn't perform. The better team won on the day.

There was no time to dwell on the defeat as Leeds flew to Salonika to face AC Milan in the European Cup-Winners Cup final. Revie was forced to shuffle his team due to the enforced absence through suspension of Bremner and Clarke and the with-drawal of Giles and Gray through injury. If that was not bad enough, preparations were jolted before the game by newspaper reports saying Don Revie was about to join Everton. The *Yorkshire Post* reported that Revie had told his players he was 95 per cent certain he would go, which could have done little for team moral before a major final.

Next stop Salonika.

AC Milan v. Leeds United, European Cup-Winners Cup final:

AC MILAN: Veechi, Sabadini, Zignoli, Anquilletti, Turone, Rosato (Dolci), Sogliano, Benetti, Bigon, Rivera, Chiarugi

LEEDS UNITED: Harvey, Reaney (captain), Cherry, Bates, Yorath, Hunter, Lorimer, Jordan, Jones, F Gray (McQueen), Madeley

Under-strength and unsure of the immediate future, Leeds players went out to face an Italian side determined to unsettle their opponents from the start. A goal behind within three minutes, Leeds' fate was sealed by a scandalous performance from the referee. Some of Christos Michas decisions were unbelievable; his bias towards the Italians outrageous, especially when turning down three blatant penalties for Leeds, who ended the match with ten players after Norman Hunter was sent off after retaliating to one blatant tackle too many. The Italian player went unpunished. Michas never officiated in a professional match again.

It was a tragic end to a season for Leeds that had a month earlier promised so much. Don Revie had never been more proud of his team, who although lacking a number of key players had outplayed AC Milan in every department. Revie lamented. 'How

Double cup disaster!

many times has this happened to us? There was the West Brom affair … the Wolves match last season. We played so well tonight and got nothing for it.'

The players won enormous praise for their efforts.

Derek Wallis, *Daily Mirror*: 'For a team to go out for such a crucial match stripped of four great players and challenge a team of Milan's status so nearly successfully was nothing short of miraculous … Unfortunately there was only heartbreak for Leeds and another heartbreak for Revie … from players who gave him everything they had and more … The catcalls, barracking and general disapproval continued as Milan took the trophy on a lap of honour. Rather it should be a lap of dishonour. The crowd was prepared to forgive Hunter's action when he retaliated … they were not prepared to forgive and forget Milan's cynicism in the form of provocative challenges as the game approached its end.'

I loved playing in Europe. Everything was organised to the last detail to make the journey as easy as possible. Whenever we played in an Iron Curtain country we took our own food to reduce the risk of health problems. We were so experienced by now that we knew most of the gamesmanship tricks European clubs used to seek an advantage, but that was all part of playing in Europe and I enjoyed the challenge.

We battled hard to face AC Milan in the European Cup-Winners Cup final and felt confident despite being without a few key players. The day before the final Don informed us all of his intention to join Everton, which rocked the boat a bit. It was a funny time to announce it, but it was about to hit the papers. All you ask in a final is an even chance. Milan were cynical, which was difficult enough to cope with, but the refereeing became farcical. Michas was banned afterwards following bribery allegations but I have always maintained that I would rather be on the losing side, rather than win by default. There's no achievement in that at all. The reception we received from the Greek supporters afterwards was incredible, but it didn't take away the disappointment afterwards in the dressing room. Losing two major cup finals in a few days was terrible, but I knew that we could pick ourselves up again.

During the season Paul boosted his tally of England caps by five. After a World Cup qualification match against Wales, Paul helped England to a memorable win against Scotland in a game to celebrate their Centenary.

Scotland v. England, Scottish FA Centenary

ENGLAND: Shilton (Leicester City), Storey (Arsenal), Hughes (Liverpool), Bell (Manchester City), Madeley (Leeds United), Moore (West Ham, captain), Ball (Arsenal), Channon (Southampton), Chivers (Tottenham Hotspur), Clarke (Leeds United), Peters (Tottenham Hotspur)

The Scots didn't enjoy it particularly because we won 5-0 on a rock-hard surface. The Scots boys were pretty quiet the following day at Elland Road, especially Peter (Lorimer) as he scored an own goal!

It was in this match that I partnered the great Bobby Moore, the only time I had the honour. He won his 100th cap in this match and was some player; his reading of the game was just magnificent. Bobby was such an inspirational player: there is more to choosing a captain than people realise. In the dressing room he was fairly quiet, but the manner in which he walked out onto the pitch I found inspirational. He had an aura about him as he led us out. You knew that he had been there, seen it and done it all over so many years. It was quite something to play alongside him.

At the end of the season Paul played in the Home Internationals before travelling with England on their post-season tour.

The most crucial game was against Poland in Chorzow. We lost 2-0, which meant England had to win the return at Wembley to qualify for the World Cup finals. In the other games of the tour we drew with Czechoslovakia 1-1, defeated USSR 2-1 and lost to Italy 2-0. It had been a disappointing end to the season, but our fate was in our hands.

Playing for England was a terrific honour. Naturally though it takes a while to get used to the demands of international football, because you're not used to the strengths and weak-

England duty for Allan Clarke, Paul, Norman Hunter and Les Cocker.

England, 1973 Home International and post-season tour squad. From left to right, back row: Hunter, Blockley, Summerbee, Clarke, Hughes, Clemence, Parkes, Shilton, Bell, McFarland, Moore, Chivers, Peters, Shepardson (trainer). Front row: Madeley, Macdonald, Storey, Ball, Channon, Richards, Nish, Keegan, Currie.

Alf's boys are ready for action.

Checkmate! England scrape a draw with a last-minute equaliser from Allan Clarke.

nesses of your teammates. However, with the likes of Moore, Banks, Charlton, Ball, Hurst and Peters in the side you soon settled in.

Throughout my career I analysed my playing ability because far too often people are not critical enough at times in terms of strengths and weaknesses. I always felt that I was only average in the air and not the best of tacklers, however I was super fit, could run non-stop, read the game and was always confident that I would not get caught out of position.

As a defender, reading the game was essential. Bobby Moore was a prime example of that. Bobby was quite slow compared to other defenders, but he was a super reader of the game and anticipated danger brilliantly. Players can sharpen up and improve their game, but certain players have a basic instinct for the game. Bobby had that in abundance, especially with his positional play, which he demonstrated on numerous occasions, especially for England, most famously in the 1966 World Cup and in his classy display against Brazil in 1970.

On our return after all the exertions of a hectic season I was ready for a break with the family, and I also helped out in the family business, which was expanding rapidly.

Time to relax with the boys,
Jason with baby Nick.

Business is booming.

Chapter Ten

CHAMPIONS ... AGAIN

1973/74

During the 1973/74 close season there was a lot of speculation surrounding the future of manager Don Revie. After seemingly deciding to take on the challenge of managing Everton, Revie had a change of heart, much to the relief of the squad he had built. Even with Revie still at the helm though, the general consensus in the media (particularly outside Leeds) was that his side in the main was a spent force, despite a number of youngsters breaking into the first-team squad.

One report highlighted the defeat by Sunderland as the final blow to Don Revie's great side. 'Sunderland smashed the most consistent team of the last decade such a shattering blow to pride, composure and self-respect that the cracks will not be easily repaired. It may well be that Leeds can never completely recover this time; can never climb back to where they were, what they were.'

Responding to the criticism in the press, Don Revie warned 'We shall not crack! Any successful club is bound to have people waiting in the wings for them to crack. We are very conscious of this at Leeds, but it acts as a challenge to prove we can still do it. So many folk say our team is growing old together and soon it must fall apart. What they forget is the side averages around 26, and I've brought in new blood.

When Terry Cooper broke his leg I brought Trevor Cherry from Huddersfield; Terry Yorath and Mick Bates were also introduced. And Joe Jordan, who cost £15,000 from Morton, was capped three times for Scotland this summer. He's 21 and is a player to watch. With Mick Jones, I reckon Leeds will have two of the best strikers in the business, and soon they'll all be talking about Frankie Gray, Eddie's brother who is only 19, and Gordon McQueen, who cost me £25,000.'

We knew what the papers had written and were determined to show everyone that we weren't finished. Youngsters were coming through and we were very experienced. Down the years we'd had a number of setbacks. Whenever we were up against it, we were at our most dangerous. Before the opening game at home to Everton, Don went through our match tactics at the team meeting in the players' lounge before telling us that he believed we were capable of going through an entire season unbeaten. Of course he was trying to motivate us, but we were a little taken aback because Don was deadly serious.

Leeds began their League campaign in sensational style, winning their opening seven games against Everton 3-1, Arsenal 2-1, Tottenham 3-0, Wolves 4-1, Birmingham

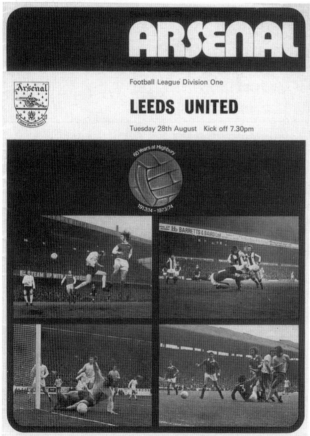

Above: Leeds United, 1973/74. From left to right, back row: Lorimer, E. Gray, Bates, Clarke, Hunter, McQueen, Ellam, Reaney, F. Gray. Front row: Yorath, Sprake, Cherry, Jordan, Giles, Harvey, Madeley, Bremner (captain), Jones.

Left: Off to a flyer ... including a clinching strike from Paul at Highbury.

3-0, Wolves 2-0 and Southampton 2-1. The win against Wolves created a club record sixth consecutive victory from the start of the season.

We began the season brilliantly and I managed to get a goal in our first away game of the season at Arsenal. Peter scored our opening goal with a free kick that had so much power it went straight through the wall. Bob Wilson never saw it and didn't move; he had no chance. I managed to score our second, but it was a bit fortuitous. I recall playing a one-two with John Giles, who flicked it over a defender. After it bounced I volleyed it with my left-foot. It was going wide, until it hit Jeff Blockley.

Southern pundits once again eulogised about Leeds as did opposing managers ...

Bill Nicholson, Tottenham Hotspur: 'Leeds are the best side in the League. I particularly admire the way they constantly support each other.' Freddie Goodwin, Birmingham City: 'Leeds will take an awful lot of stopping. They are better than England in some ways. Here you've got an all-international outfit with the wonderful blend that comes from playing together for so long.'

The winning run ended when Manchester United gained a draw with an ultra-defensive display at Elland Road, but the unbeaten run continued. As Leeds ploughed forward in the League, Paul prepared himself for England's crunch match in the World Cup qualifying group against Poland, initially with a friendly against Austria.

We warmed up against Austria and destroyed them 7-0. We had a good balance to the side and felt extremely confident going into the match at Wembley. Alf kept the same side for the Poland clash. The expectancy was incredible, but we knew that we were capable of winning.

Poland v. England, World Cup qualifying round

ENGLAND: Shilton (Leicester City), Madeley (Leeds United), Hughes (Liverpool), Bell (Manchester City), McFarland (Derby County), Hunter (Leeds United), Currie (Sheffield United), Channon (Southampton), Chivers (Tottenham Hotspur), Clarke (Leeds United), Peters (Tottenham Hotspur, captain)

The Poland clash has gone down as one of the most frustrating nights in English football's history. No England supporter present or watching on television will ever forget the Polish goalkeeper Jan Tomachesky's performance or, sadly, Norman Hunter's 'missed' tackle in the build-up to Poland's crucial goal!

The atmosphere in the ground was sensational, but the match turned into one of those frustrating nights when the ball just would not go in, although Allan scored a late penalty. Their 'keeper Tomachesky was nicknamed the clown by television pundits, but he was astonishing. Some of the saves he pulled off were beyond belief. It was just incredible that none of the chances we made went in, and of course everyone remembers the game for Norman's error, but the media treated him harshly afterwards. Poland were fortunate on the night, but they were no pushovers as they proved in the finals when they finished third. A few weeks later we lost at home to Italy 1-0 in a friendly. It proved to be my last game of the season for England and Bobby Moore's last for his country to end his illustrious international career. Alf would also soon lose his job.

Back on the domestic front, hard-fought wins against Liverpool and at Manchester City, both by a solitary goal, were followed by an exhilarating performance against West Ham, which Leeds won 4–1. Only a third of the season may have gone, but Leeds were already six points clear of their nearest challengers.

Following the clash against Liverpool (a Mick Jones header winning a pulsating match), Red Star Belgrade coach Milan Milanic, thought Jones' goal 'was skilfully worked and brilliantly scored … a goal reminiscent of Garrincha and Pele at work for

Arrivederchi … the great Bobby Moore retires.

Merry Xmas everybody ... It certainly was at Elland Road.

Brazil.' West Ham boss Ron Greenwood was convinced the title race was all but over. 'Leeds are the equal of Manchester United in their heyday. They play with such skill, imagination and flair. It looks as if they are out on their own, playing the sort of football I would love to play.'

The confidence was back in our side. It didn't matter who we played, we believed we could win.

As Christmas approached, following a 2-2 draw with QPR, consecutive wins over Ipswich Town, Chelsea, Norwich City and Newcastle United saw Leeds go nine points clear of the chasing pack. The team's 2-1 win at Stamford Bridge set a post-war record of twenty games unbeaten from the start of a Football League campaign.

Against Ipswich Town, prior to the game, their manager Bobby Robson popped in to welcome us and saw Gordon McQueen warming up in the dressing room. Gordon had broken into the side and was making a name for himself, he was doing some standing jumps and you could see him disappearing behind the skylight. The look on Bobby's face was incredible, you could see him thinking, who is this they're unleashing on us! Ipswich were on the up at the time, but we won 3-0.

Bob Cass wrote following the Boxing Day clash at Newcastle: 'A packed crowd came and saw their team not only conquered, but fairly ground into the pitch by the remorseless skill of the heir apparents to the league title. And if any of them were still wondering who could halt this relentless march of Don Revie's men surely none would regard it as little more than a pause on their way to greatness. The goal –

Boxing Day bliss ... Paul grabs another winner.

Madeley pushed the ball forward before letting loose with an awesome right-foot shot from 30 yards that the 'keeper could only push into the net.'

The strike against Newcastle was a nice present for the lads! In the dressing room afterwards Don joked with their manager that they needed a new goalkeeper.

Following a draw at Birmingham City bookmakers refused to take bets on Leeds winning the title, however you could get 25-1 against the team remaining undefeated for the rest of the season!

We were losing at Birmingham when Joe Jordan scored with only a few minutes to go which preserved our unbeaten record. I played a long ball to Peter who set up Joe with a great cross. At the time, publicly we said there was no pressure whilst we were on the record run, but when you're out there you want to keep it going as long as you can. The result at St Andrews although a draw, felt more like a win.

Leeds' utility man makes the programme cover but it was Joe Jordan who gave Birmingham the Blues!

Playing with panache and a swagger, the team was receiving national acclaim.

Frank McGhee *Mirror*: 'Leeds are in grave danger of being more admired, acclaimed and loved more universally than this much-maligned team would have dared to dream a few years back.'

Terry McNeil believed that if a manager had the gift of being able to sign any player; Madeley would be their choice. 'They would die with a smile on their faces, for Leeds' play-anywhere defender has emerged as Britain's most-wanted player.'

With every team desperate to beat Leeds, each match became more intense. The New Year began with three draws in four games, the only victory coming against Southampton, before consecutive wins over Arsenal and Manchester United took the run to 29 games undefeated. Leeds were now within a match of equalling the record unbeaten run from the beginning of a Division One campaign, set by Burnley in 1920/21.

Before their clash with Stoke City though, Leeds attention focused on the FA Cup and a fifth-round clash against Bristol City. Having been eliminated from the League

Paul battles away with Bristol City forward Tainton as Leeds go out of the FA Cup.

Cup and UEFA Cup at an early stage, Leeds were now favourites to lift the FA Cup and complete the 'double'. However, following a 1-1 draw at Aston Gate, their plucky opponents shocked them with a 1-0 win at Elland Road.

Free to 'concentrate on the League' the only danger to ultimate success was the number of injuries the team was picking up. John Giles had missed much of the campaign and Eddie Gray was out for the season. The latest casualty was now Mick Jones (his injury would end his career) on the eve of their clash with Stoke City. Although Leeds took a two-goal lead, Stoke battled back to win 3-2, ex-Leeds player Jimmy Greenhoff scoring the winning goal. It was the start of a worrying spell that would bring just one win in seven games, including four defeats. The fourth loss was at West Ham and there was a real danger that the title may slip away because Liverpool could mathematically overhaul Leeds if they won all their games in hand.

We'd had an incredible run, but suddenly began to struggle. Injuries were beginning to take their toll, but we were still top, even though our only challengers Liverpool could overtake us. There was only one thing we could do, battle away.

During a nerve-wracking few games, Leeds earned a hard-fought win against Derby County as Liverpool dropped points in two of their matches in hand. Leeds were back in control of their own destiny, but only just as draws at Coventry and against Sheffield United at Elland Road, where an appalling decision by the referee denied Leeds a vital victory, meant that Liverpool could tie on points, although Leeds' goal average was superior. However, there was no room for any more slips.

The win against Derby was crucial, and once again Billy, playing as an emergency striker, came up trumps with a great finish. Over the years, decisions had cost us dearly. Against Sheffield, Allan had strayed offside when Peter scored, but there was no way he was interfering with play. We were not happy after the match, but our destiny was still in our hands.

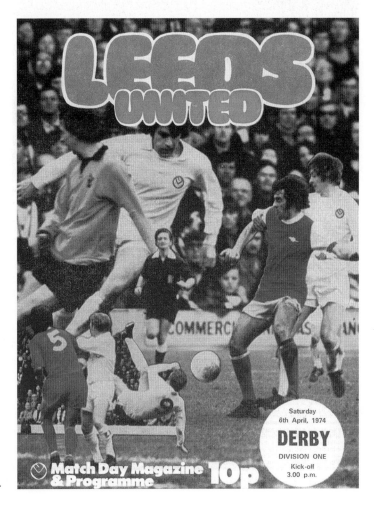

A must-win game.

Well done skipper … Billy grabs a vital goal.

Twenty-four hours after their controversial clash with Yorkshire-rivals Sheffield United, Leeds made the short journey to Bramall Lane where they faced a hostile crowd, and a team desperate to end their Championship challenge. Don Revie sprung a surprise by recalling Mick Jones, though only half fit. With Liverpool winning 4-0 at half-time against Manchester City, the pressure was on Leeds. They simply had to win. Drawing on all their reserves, two goals after the break from Peter Lorimer proved crucial. Revie's gamble proved a masterstroke as Jones made both goals in Leeds' 2-0 victory. The win was vital and local papers were ecstatic with the result.

Terry Brindle, *Yorkshire Post*: 'If resilience, determination and sheer fighting spirit can win Championships, when form and fluency has been drained, then Leeds United will wrest the League title from Liverpool in 10 days time. Leeds' victory, amid the high drama of Bramall Lane last night, was a triumph for endeavour over the frustrations and threatening disappointment of a strangely contrasting season. It was a triumph for the commitment and character which keeps Leeds going long after bone and muscle ought to have rebelled … against never-ending pressure.'

Leeds' penultimate match of the season was against Ipswich Town, which would not be for the faint-hearted! Leeds began brightly, taking a two–goal lead to settle everyone's nerves in the ground, but Ipswich to their credit played themselves back into the match. When they equalised the tension was palpable. Cometh the hour, 'Sniffer' Clarke poached a late goal to win the game 3-2.

Allan had a habit of scoring important goals and his late strike was one of his most crucial. It was a wonderful moment. The feeling in the dressing room afterwards was one of great relief because we only needed a draw in our final match against Queens Park Rangers to clinch the title whatever Liverpool did in their final games.

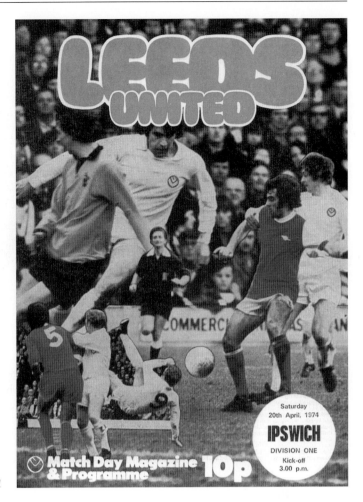

Crunch time!

After the game Revie admitted he feared the worst after Ipswich equalised. However, he wasn't celebrating just yet. 'It's a bit premature to call us Champions. I'll not breathe easily until I see the trophy in Billy Bremner's hands.' The papers weren't so tentative ...

Tom Holley, *The People*: 'This victory could bring the First Division title to Elland Road, and on this display by United it's just as well. Even though they swept into a two-goal lead they never settled down to play anything like their old confidence and flair. Their defence stayed tense and anxious, their midfield trio never really got on top of their job and their forwards were rarely able to put the Ipswich defence under any real pressure'

Barry Foster *Yorkshire Post*: 'Almost there. That is how Leeds United must feel this morning ... the odds on Leeds taking their second League title swung very heavily towards Elland Road.'

Before Leeds' last game Liverpool faced Arsenal at Anfield midweek, but they cracked under the pressure. Their 1-0 defeat handed Leeds the title. Leeds were Champions once again ...

Leeds defend a corner in a gripping encounter.

I was at home when the result came through that we'd won the Championship. After a few calls all the players met up for a celebration drink, it was some night.

After guiding Leeds to a second Championship, Don Revie believed this triumph was the greatest achievement during his thirteen years as manager. In an interview with the *Yorkshire Evening Post*, Revie summed up his feelings on a quite outstanding season:

I really do think this win is a greater achievement than the first one. When we won the First Division title last time we were able to keep a more settled formation. This season we have had to overcome a tremendous amount of switching about because of numerous injury setbacks. In some games we have had to play without as many as five internationals. It speaks volumes for the players who have come into the side and helped us so well that we have been able to win the title. I simply cannot praise my players enough. They have worked tremendously hard throughout the season and I feel they have deserved the reward, which has now come their way. I am proud of them all.

I feel as though someone has come along and lifted six tons of coal off my back. It's a great feeling. After we lost at Stoke and Liverpool, at home to Burnley and down at West Ham, everyone said we were cracking up. I thought then that there was a chance of Liverpool being able to catch us, but the players got their heads down, put their heart and soul into their play and in the period around Easter we managed to take six points out of eight available. At the same time we did not concede one goal. That to me showed the tremendous ability and character of the players we have at Elland Road. Never was the test greater than it was at that time, but they came through it well.

Liverpool manager Bill Shankly was magnanimous in his praise for the victors, as he had been in 1969. 'Leeds United are truly great champions. I know that Leeds care about everyone, from the cleaning ladies right through, and that is how it should be.'

Leeds won their final game of the season 1-0 with another clinical strike from Allan Clarke. Once again the players had proved they were the best in England. With the pressure off, Leeds relaxed and played like champions. Ken Jones wrote: 'What a difference a week made to Leeds. They were off the hook in London and they loved it.

Time to relax.

Champions at last they celebrated in style, treating us to the extravagances which had to be buried on sterner occasions.'

Leeds United League record: P42 W 24 D 14 L 4 F 66 A 31 Pts 62

Player appearances during the season (substitute in brackets): Harvey 39, Reaney 36, Cherry 37 (1), Bremner 42, McQueen 36, Hunter 42, Lorimer 37, Clarke 34, Jones 28 (3), Giles 17, Madeley 39, Jordan 25 (8), Yorath 23 (5), E. Gray 8, Bates 9 (1), F. Gray 3 (3), Ellam 3 (1), Cooper (1) 1, Stewart 3, Liddell (1)

Goals: Jones 14, Clarke 13, Lorimer 12, Bremner 10, Jordan 7, Madeley 2, Giles 2, Yorath 2, Bates 2, Cherry 1, Own Goal 1.

During the close season Don Revie left to manage England. His tenure at the club had seen the club rise from oblivion to the very top. Apart from John Giles, Mick Jones and Allan Clarke every player had come through the ranks, creating a 'family' atmosphere unrivalled in the club's history. Guiding Leeds to the Division One Championship twice, they had also finished runners-up on five occasions and never finished out of the top four since winning the Division Two title in 1963/64. In addition, during this period they reached four FA Cup finals, a League Cup final and four European finals – a record no English team could match during this period.

His squad had become international stars, and the younger players who had broken into the side would go on to represent their country with distinction. Don Revie masterminded a golden era at Elland Road which meant that his players' achievements would always be compared to that of future teams. His legacy will stand forever.

Looking back, winning the first title was 'sweeter' than our second because we achieved it ourselves on the night. In '74 Liverpool's defeat to Arsenal handed us the title. Of course we'd put the work in, but winning it by your own efforts on the day captured the moment instantly. That said, it was wonderful to be Champions again.

When Don left it was very disappointing because I'd never known another manager, but I never felt let down. He'd been great to me down the years, but it was obviously the end of an era and we all knew the team would soon be breaking up. Everybody has to make their own choices in life and if he felt that was best for him, then that was fine by me. I didn't think that he owed anything to the players there, we all owed more to him.

The atmosphere at Leeds since I arrived at the club was fantastic. We were all one family, which was down to Don Revie. Everybody behind the scenes mattered – the laundry ladies, stewards, and cleaners. Don had so many strengths, but for me his man-management skills shone through. He always got the best out of us. We had a big squad of exceptionally talented players, which he managed to keep happy, whether you were in the first team or on the periphery. I don't recall players asking to leave. Everyone knew we were at a successful side and wanted to be part of it. He knew when to give a player a kick up the backside or put an arm around them for encouragement.

Simply the best!

We are the Champions ... again.

'Double' champ!

I always felt that I was playing for him, more so than for my family or myself, however strange that may seem. I wanted to repay the faith he had shown in me not just as a young boy when we started but throughout his years as manager. We had an incredible spirit of defiance and determination. It was just such a pleasure to be at Elland Road and it was so enjoyable. Whether we were training or travelling, nothing was too much trouble for his players. He made everyone feel wanted, players and back room staff alike.

There was something about him that made you want to strive that bit more. The way he handled us all was superb. A word of encouragement, a nod of approval or a compliment on the way you played in the previous game. He had a knack of making you feel ten feet tall. During a match day team-talk Don would pick out the key points from the dossier that had been prepared. People said we had to study them, that's nonsense. Syd Owen and Maurice Lindley watched the opposition and compiled the strengths, weaknesses and tactical information. Don simply gave us instructions on whom the danger men were and what to look out for set-piece-wise.

Tactically, we knew whom we had to mark defensively and attacking-wise we practised corners and free kicks, but generally kept it simple. Normally Peter would smack it in, so players would look for rebounds, or we'd chip it for Big Jack, Mick or Allan depending on the position of the set play. There wasn't a fantastic variety, because during the course of a match we had the players who could alter the pattern of play. We could pick up the pace or slow it down depending on the circumstances. Possession football was no problem to us, and if we had to mix it we would.

The only thing I never understood about Don was his superstitious nature. All the players had the odd superstition: what order they put their strip on or lined up when we went out, but Don was in a different league. At one time he wore a 'lucky' blue suit to every match. In later years Don said he should have let us just go out and express ourselves earlier than we did, but its difficult to criticise because we were incredibly successful in our era. No team at the time matched our achievements or consistency, and no Leeds team since has come close either. His departure was truly the end of an era.

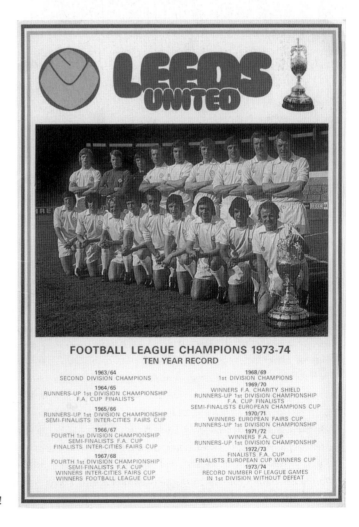

The glory years!

Chapter Eleven

BAYERN BLUES

1974/75

During the close season Paul returned to his roots to open a new clubhouse at Farsley Celtic, but throughout the summer one story surrounded Leeds United... who would replace Don Revie as manager?

It was a tremendous honour returning to Farsley Celtic and seeing how the club had developed since my days as a player with the club. You were unable though to get away from the intense speculation on Don's successor. We'd been so successful it was always going to be a tough decision. When Brian Clough got the job as manager I was surprised because he had been so critical over the years about us. He was the last manager I expected to take over. John Giles was Don's choice; Billy also expressed an interest. As it turned out neither got the job. When we reported back for training Brian was still on holiday, which was a bit surprising, but nothing prepared us for his first team-talk when he had a go at us all. There was a stunned silence. We'd been together years as a team, offending us really hurt. He lost the players' respect instantly. Brian arrived at Leeds at the wrong time, with the wrong group of players for his management style.

Leeds opened their season at Wembley in the Charity Shield (Leeds losing to Liverpool 6-5 in a penalty shoot out after a 1-1 draw). Paul missed the match due to injury, but was back for the first League game of the season at Stoke City as they began their title defence. Their 3-0 defeat was the start of their worst opening to a League campaign for a decade. Brian Clough was sacked after just 44 turbulent days.

Morale was really low. After our worst start since I arrived at the club we had a crisis meeting within a few games. Brian was given a vote of no confidence and Jimmy Armfield soon replaced him. Results quickly improved as the team settled. In his brief spell Brian had added to the squad, but only one player stayed, Duncan McKenzie.

The appointment of Jimmy Armfield, with Don Howe as first-team coach, had the desired effect. Leeds climbed away from the bottom of the table and produced some fine results, including wins over Sheffield United, West Ham and Arsenal to eventually finish ninth.

In the FA Cup, Leeds accounted for Cardiff City, Southern League giant-killers Wimbledon and Derby before going out of the competition at the quarter-final stage

Home sweet home! Paul opens the new clubhouse at his old club, Farsley Celtic.

Leeds United, 1974/75. From left to right, back row: Madeley, Hunter, Cherry, Jordan, McQueen, Stewart, Harvey, E. Gray, Clarke, Reaney. Front row: Lorimer, Giles, Bremner (captain), Cooper, Bates, F. Gray, Yorath.

Above: A future Leeds star Tony Currie just misses with this strike but his team is thumped 5-1.

Left: West Ham take the lead, but Leeds bounce back to win.

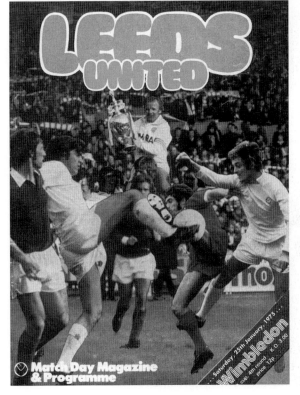

No way through for Cardiff City striker Showers as Leeds march on in the FA Cup.

Left: Bring on the Wombles!

Left: Is this Dickie Guy in disguise?!

Below: On the Buses … It may be a publicity shot but Frank Gray, Paul Reaney, Mick Bates, Terry Cooper, Trevor Cherry, Eddie Gray, Terry Yorath, John O'Hare, Mick Jones and Duncan Mckenzie are happy to oblige.

All smiles as the team prepare for cup battles at home and in Europe.

to Ipswich Town in a tie that went to three replays. The clash against Wimbledon caught the public's imagination, and is best remembered because Dickie Guy saved a late penalty from Peter Lorimer in the first leg at Elland Road to earn his side a famous draw. Leeds eventually knocked the 'Wombles' out courtesy of an own goal in the replay.

A few weeks after bowing out of the competition, Paul played in England's side at Wembley that thrashed Cyprus 5-0. This was the third cap awarded to him by Sir Alf Ramsey's successor Don Revie during England's European Championship campaign. Paul had contributed to a 3-0 win against Czechoslovakia before playing in his country's 0-0 draw with Portugal.

> *It was great to be back in the squad and teaming up with Don again. I played in his first two matches in charge, before we hammered Cyprus. Malcolm Macdonald scored all five goals (a post-war record), which was some performance.*

Away from the domestic scene, Leeds had played with confidence throughout their European Cup campaign, their years of experience helping them ease past FC Zurich, Ujpesti Dozsa and Anderlecht before they faced Spanish giants Barcelona in the semi-finals.

> *We performed well in the early rounds prior to being drawn to play a very good Barcelona team. They had some world-class players in their side including Johann Cryuff and Johann*

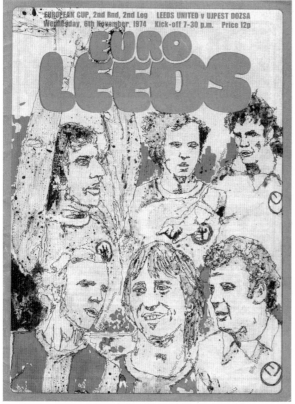

Above: Muddy heroes ... Leeds reach the FA Cup quarter-finals.

Left: Psychedelic design for Leeds' European Cup match programmes!

Paul keeps the world's best player Johann Cruyff in his sights during a thrilling first leg at Elland Road.

Neeskens. After winning the home leg 2-1, the key moment for me was Peter Lorimer's goal in the away leg early in the first half. A 3-1 lead was substantial and we didn't give too many chances away, even though Gordon McQueen got sent off. When they did get a shot on target Dave Stewart (another of my ex-roommates) had an inspired game. Although they equalised on the night, we were through to the final on aggregate 3-2. After the game the scenes in the dressing room were ecstatic, although Gordon had his head in his hands knowing he'd be missing the final. His dismissal guaranteed my place but I knew we'd miss his aerial power, because I'm sure he'd have caused Bayern Munich problems at both ends. That was for the future though. We'd worked years for this moment and savoured every minute. It was a very special night.

The ultimate prize awaits …

Bayern Munich v. Leeds United, European Cup final

BAYERN MUNICH: Maier, Durnberger, Andersson (sub Weiss), Schwarzenbech, Beckenbauer (captain), Roth, Tortensson, Zobel, Muller, Hoeness (sub Wunder), Kapellmann

LEEDS UNITED: Stewart, Reaney, F. Gray, Bremner (captain), Madeley, Hunter, Lorimer, Clarke, Jordan, Giles, Yorath (sub E. Gray)

Leeds arrived in Paris feeling quietly confident.

Bayern had some great players in their side. When I first saw Franz Beckenbauer play in the sweeper role I'd never seen anything like it before. He dictated play from behind the back three or four, deciding when to stroll forward and hit crisp 40 or 50-yard passes. By the time I played against him he'd reverted to centre-half and oozed class. Another star was the goal machine Gerd Muller. For 89 minutes he would do nothing then strike; he was such a natural goal-scorer. Muller had the knack of just tapping the ball and it would go in.

Sadly for Leeds, in the biggest game in their history, although they dictated play for long periods, fate would conspire against them at the most critical time.

We dominated play for long periods and did more than enough to win, but as on previous occasions refereeing decisions cost us dearly. Two incidents stood out. First, when Beckenbauer blatantly brought down Allan for a penalty, which the referee somehow missed when placed just yards away, then in the second half when Peter had a fabulous strike harshly chalked off when Billy was adjudged to have strayed offside. Each incident was a devastating body blow. Bayern, who had hardly threatened throughout the game grabbed two goals from counter-attacks, one from Muller who I was marking. He'd barely touched the ball until the end when he scored.

I was so disappointed because I really thought we'd win that night. After all the near misses down the years, I thought everything would finally come right and we'd win the biggest prize of all. A European Cup would have been the crowning glory, but it wasn't to be.

I enjoyed the challenge of playing in Europe. You had to overcome different tactics and styles of play. Some opponents were incredibly skilful, others unbelievably cynical and play-acted at every opportunity, but we overcame them and had a great record. During my campaigns in Europe, Leeds reached five finals, of which I only missed one. They were great days, but we all realised that the club was about to enter a transitional phase. It was the end of an era for the team.

It doesn't get bigger than this. The 1975 European Cup final.

Muller breaks Leeds hearts with Bayern Munich's second goal.

End of a dream and an era.

Chapter Twelve

END OF THE ROAD

1975-1981

During the 1975/76 close-season John Giles joined West Brom as player-manager. As Revie's aces moved on, new heroes began to emerge including the mercurial Duncan McKenzie who established himself in the side with Joe Jordan injured for the opening half of the season. As for Paul Madeley, he partnered Norman Hunter in central defence with Gordon McQueen out with a long-term injury.

I was obviously sorry to see the lads slowly depart, but it was inevitable that at some stage the team would break up. Following Don was always going to be hard during the previous campaign, I recall Jimmy Armfield leaving John out of several big games, which made him most unhappy. He let his feelings be known by blowing dust off his boots! Jimmy had to make tough decisions and of course John was a legend at Leeds, so it could not have been easy to omit him. Duncan was a real extrovert and had great individual ability; the fans loved him. At times he could score the most fantastic goals, he was a real crowd-pleaser, but he was also difficult to play with because he was such a maverick. Before a game Billy would roll the ball to him in the dressing room and say, tongue in cheek, 'Duncan, that's a pass!' He eventually settled and scored quite a few goals during his spell at Leeds.

Leeds began the season well, winning four of their opening seven matches. The team was playing well and Paul was grabbing his share of the headlines. Following a 2-0 win at Sheffield United in August, Peter Cooper wrote:

James Bond's 'M' prefers to stay in the background. Leeds United's can't ... Paul Madeley strolled Bramall Lane as if he owned Sheffield United's new stand. Like Bond's 'M', he issued the licence to kill-off a Sheffield side who tilted at Europe last season but, alongside a supposedly faded Leeds, must feel it's as well they didn't make it. It was mainly thirty-one-year-old Madeley, busy as a teenager, who clinched a therapeutic away win. Not bad for a creaking 'old-timer' in a team of write-offs ...

Madeley's form brought him a recall back to the England side when during the autumn England played crucial games against Czechoslovakia and Poland, matches that would decide their fate in the European Championship qualifying tournament.

Leeds United, 1975/76. From left to right, back row: Armfield (manager), McKenzie, Jordan, McQueen, Harvey, Stewart, Madeley, Hunter, Reaney. Front row: Yorath, F. Gray, E. Gray, Lorimer, Cherry, Bremner (captain), Clarke.

Unfortunately, England performed poorly, losing in Bratislava 2-1 and only drawing 1-1 in Portugal to miss out on a place in the finals.

At the turn of the year seven wins in eight games saw Leeds challenging near the top. During this run Paul scored his only goal of the season, a Boxing Day special in a 1-0 win at Maine Road.

> *It was great coming up trumps with another Christmas present for the lads, this time a header at Manchester City. I was marking Joe Royle but for some reason moved into attack and anticipated Frank Gray's early cross to head home. I was really pleased.*

Playing with confidence, Leeds were considered a good outside bet for the FA Cup. After knocking out Notts County in the third round, Leeds faced Crystal Palace at Elland Road. Bob Gray in *The Weekly News* evaluated the 'new Leeds' under Jimmy Armfield:

> Leeds United are back in the old routine. Battling for the League–FA Cup 'double', Leeds have knocked back all forecasts that advancing years would blunt their competitive edge. They have shown too that they can survive injuries to internationalists Joe Jordan and Gordon McQueen. Since Madeley took over at centre-half, Leeds have conceded just six goals in eleven games. Paul has always been the quiet man of Elland Road. Even now, with a host of medals and caps

behind him and a flourishing family do-it-yourself business to boost his status, he prefers to stay out of the glare of publicity that surrounds Elland Road.

Gray then interviewed Paul Madeley about 'Life at Leeds'. Paul told the reporter:

The team has adapted to cope with big Gordon's absence. I play a 'double' centre-half role with Trevor Cherry and Norman Hunter. The other players are working hard to prevent the opposition slinging in a stream of high balls. I have had a lot of pleasure out of my football this season. Since Don Howe arrived we have had more variety in training. I really look forward to going to the ground in the morning. The secret is to keep your enthusiasm going. Don told me the other day that he sees no reason why a player can't go on in the First Division until he is thirty-six or so. As long as I keep my appetite for the game, you can make up a lost yard of speed with an extra yard of experience. That'll do for me.

The mickey-taking is ferocious. Nobody is exempt; they're always at it. When I leave the ground to go home I always put on a posh voice. Billy loves that stuff. Even the boss is at it. Ten minutes before a match he is still telling jokes in the dressing room. But that is not casual; it's deliberate. We have had all our briefings by that stage. He is aiming to break the tension, but when we leave the tunnel we are deadly serious. I see the funny side of things, but I just can't switch on and off during a game, I have to concentrate completely on what I am doing. One blink can cost you a yard, and that is fatal.

Unfortunately Palace, managed by charismatic manager Malcolm Allison, caused a major cup upset by beating Leeds 1-0. The defeat was a setback for Armfield's team, although they finished the season in a creditable fifth place.

Going out of the FA Cup was a bitter blow, because we fancied our chances of a cup run, but the season went well overall. Finishing fifth was a terrific effort during this period of transition, and to cap a great campaign I won the club's Player of the Year award.

Having missed the Home International Championships and post-season Bi-Centennial tournament in America, Paul suddenly found himself recalled to the England team to face Finland in the opening World Cup qualifying match, replacing Brian Greenhoff in the side. Revie told reporters: 'I have picked Madeley for a specific job, to mark Finland's centre forward Olavi Rissanen. When I watched him in Helsinki three weeks ago, I felt Paul was the man who might contain him. Rissanen is sharp and comes off people well. He is the player most likely to cause us problems. Paul can play well in any of the back four positions. At this job he is one of the best in the world.'

We got off to a great start with a 4-1 win, and played well. I partnered Phil Thompson of Liverpool in defence, which worked well, because he was solid in the air, enabling me to sweep up behind him. It was a great end to the season, but I was having reservations about my future international career and knew it would soon end.

Left: Top man! Player of the Year 1975/76.

Below: Time to celebrate.

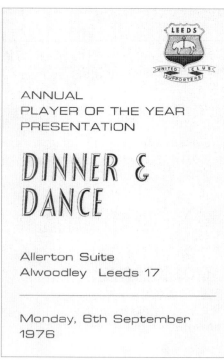

ANNUAL
PLAYER OF THE YEAR
PRESENTATION

DINNER &
DANCE

Allerton Suite
Alwoodley   Leeds 17

Monday, 6th September
1976

Within three months of the 1976/77 campaign Billy Bremner had joined Hull City and Norman Hunter had moved on to Bristol City. The season saw two mini runs that kept the team in the top ten. The best came around New Year when Leeds suffered just one defeat in a nine-match run which brought six wins, the most exciting against Middlesborough when two goals from McQueen in the last five minutes settled a thrilling match 2-1. Leeds ended the campaign in tenth place.

Only Peter Lorimer, Eddie Gray, Paul Reaney, David Harvey and myself now remained from my days as an apprentice. Don's team had developed over a number of years, so restructuring another side was always going to be a tough task for a new manager. Players came in, but however good they were it would be impossible to immediately replace a group of players who had grown up together and achieved success over a sustained period. Where Leeds was different to the likes of Manchester United, Liverpool, Arsenal, Manchester City, Everton and Tottenham was that the club had never achieved major success before, so building another successful team was going to take time.

Fans who had grown used to seeing a winning team got frustrated at times, which was understandable, but everyone tried their best. As new players came in, you accepted them for their ability. If they gave their best, you could not expect any more. Joe Jordan and Gordon McQueen had broken through towards the end of Don's era at the club and had a head start over players like Peter Hampton, Carl Harris and David McNiven. Unfortunately, whereas

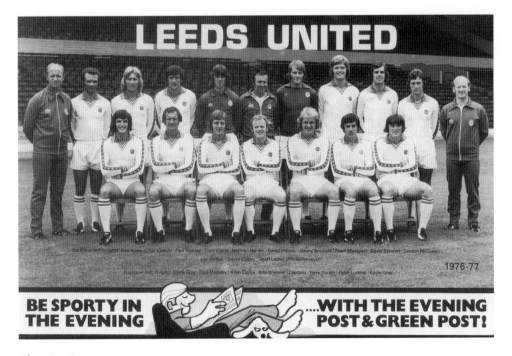

Changing times...

Paul clears his lines in this clash against Middlesbrough, a match won by two late goals from young Gordon McQueen.

Joe and Gordon went on to have exceptional careers, overall the players coming through were not up to the calibre of the ones before. Of course there were exceptions, Tony Currie, who was into his second season at Leeds, had proved an immediate hit with supporters, and would become a good investment.

Behind the scenes Jimmy Armfield created a calming influence during a difficult era in the club's history. His personality and style suited the club at the time and his organisational skills said much about his managerial ability. Jimmy was very likeable; I got on with him very well as most of the players did.

During the season Paul made his final two appearances for England, both friendly matches at Wembley, firstly against the Republic of Ireland, a match that finished 1-1, then Holland in February 1977, taking his tally of caps to 24. The Dutch were in the midst of a 'golden' era when they reached successive World Cup finals and had in their ranks the likes of Cruyff, Rep, Neeskens and Van de Kerkhof. Their style of football was exhilarating to watch, and they overcame England's challenge all too easily.

ENGLAND *v.* HOLLAND: Clemence (Liverpool), Clement (QPR), Beattie (Ipswich Town), Doyle (Manchester City), Watson (Sunderland), Madeley (Leeds United), Keegan (Liverpool, captain), Greenhoff (Manchester United), Francis (Birmingham City), Bowles (QPR), Brooking (West Ham)

Holland had some outstanding players; Johann Cruyff scored twice. He was arguably the best footballer in the world at the time, and was some player. There was no great mystery about my retirement from international football. I wanted to prolong my career at Leeds as long as possible so told Don that I did not feel playing the whole year round was doing me a lot of good. I knew that it would be better for me if I rested during the summer. For years we'd been playing two games a week, plus internationals and that takes it out of you. Resting during the summer would prolong my career.

When Don resigned from the post he received a lot of criticism, which was unfair, because succeeding Sir Alf Ramsey was always going to be an almost impossible task. Being compared to a World Cup winner meant he was on a hiding to nothing, and you only have to look at all the England managers since him to realise the difficulty of the job.

Looking back on my England career, my only regret was that we never made the '74 finals, because we had a great side. Our form was good going into the match with Poland, we unfortunately experienced one of those freakish results. You generally don't get a long career as an international player so you have to make the most of it. I was fortunate to play against all the renowned players of the era.

This is one 'Roses' battle
that Leeds couldn't conquer.

The highlight of the season for Leeds was a fine FA Cup run. Following wins over Norwich City and Birmingham City, Leeds faced a tough tie against Manchester City at Elland Road. In a cracking encounter a replay looked inevitable until Trevor Cherry popped up with a late winner. Following a 1-0 win in the quarter-finals at Wolves, Leeds drew Manchester United for a third time at the semi-final stage.

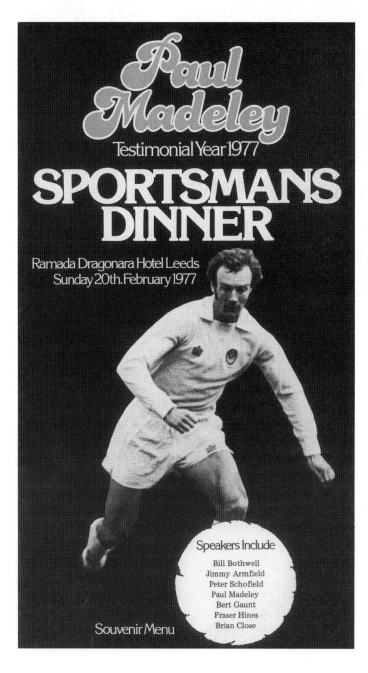

Paul Madeley
Testimonial Year 1977

SPORTSMANS DINNER

Ramada Dragonara Hotel Leeds
Sunday 20th. February 1977

Speakers Include

Bill Bothwell
Jimmy Armfield
Peter Schofield
Paul Madeley
Bert Gaunt
Fraser Hines
Brian Close

Souvenir Menu

The stars turn out for Paul during his testimonial year.

Brother's Michael and John flank Paul during a sportsman's dinner in his honour.

This was my sixth FA Cup semi-final for Leeds and I knew that it would be extremely tough. Manchester United had rebuilt their side after being relegated in 1974, and had a number of great young players like Gordon Hill, Steve Coppell and Stuart Pearson in their side. Our defeat was particularly disappointing because I felt we could and should have done better. They caught us early on with two quick goals, and we were always chasing the game afterwards. We managed to get one goal back but it was too late. The dressing room was really down afterwards because we under-performed.

The season was also notable for Paul in that he was awarded a testimonial, following Jack Charlton, Billy Bremner, Norman Hunter and Paul Reaney before him. Following a tribute dinner at the Dragonara Hotel, Leeds faced the full Republic of Ireland XI, managed by his former team-mate and now player–manager John Giles, 26 March 1977. Prior to the match Giles paid tribute to his former colleague in the *Yorkshire Evening Post*:

If I ever had to pick a 'dream' team Paul's name would be one of the first to write down ... in about seven different positions! Paul is one of the most mobile

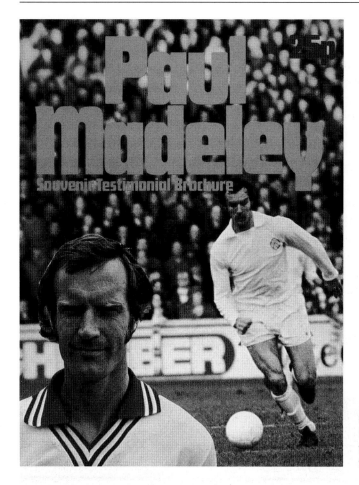

Souvenir brochure as a Republic of Ireland XI take on Leeds in Paul's testimonial game.

players I've ever seen and it was this mobility and his general quickness, which enabled him to play in so many positions. He's also one of the nicest people you could wish to meet. Without him, and when Paul was substitute it was like having seven different players in one shirt, and Leeds would not have been quite as invincible over the years. Paul was a truly world-class player.

Don Revie recalled first seeing Paul play in his early days as manager when Leeds were scouring local leagues for talent.

The tall, elegant youngster wearing the number 6 shirt stood out whichever way you looked at him. He had grace, poise and control ... Everything he did seemed to indicate he had that quality all managers search for but so infrequently find.

Paul has been, over the years, one of the finest players in the world. There are few players who have had his ability in defensive roles and few players who have had the ability to adapt so brilliantly to every position on the field.

Wherever he played he'd give the sort of performance you'd expect from someone who'd played in that position for years. Week in, week out, he was flawless, and what a professional. You always knew he would give you a great performance when it mattered. No professional footballer is as respected by opponents as Paul. You rarely notice him because he's so good.

We christened him the 'Rolls-Royce' of football, and how better could you describe him? We used to smile when Paul broke away with the ball and started to move forward. Opponents would try to run him but we used to say it was like watching a Rolls slip into overdrive and glide effortlessly and unflappably away leaving everyone else in hot pursuit.

The day I signed him was one of the best day's work I ever did for Leeds United. Paul is one of the finest players in the world because in every aspect of the game, apart from putting the ball in the back of the net, he's world class. Paul was as much responsible for the successes over the years as anyone else was. The club and fans owe him a lot for his loyalty and dedication. Paul is dedicated, he is loyal and he is a complete professional ... Paul Madeley is quite simply one of the best in the world.

As for Paul, he felt he'd been lucky that his career had been spent at the top of English football.

Good luck!

Most of us came into the side together and we had an ideal blend. We always had tremen-dous pride in ourselves and it spurred us on time and again after our setbacks. We couldn't have done it without the basic ability, and we had the best manager in the game. Even the opposing fans who used to turn up in their thousands to watch us lose on our travels merely used to make us try harder.

We were truly a family, together for such a long time and experiencing every possible foot-balling emotion. Until this season we had played more European games than any other English side. We had more than a decade of glory with virtually the same team, won every domestic trophy and were in the finals of all three European competitions.

Looking back, it seems strange that we invariably seemed on the wrong end of refereeing decisions in key matches, like the European Cup-Winners Cup and European Cup finals, but its better to have got there, than to have failed to get there at all. I have no regrets. I've had more success than 99 per cent of all other professional footballers in the country and the game has given me everything.

Leeds began the 1977/78 season poorly but hit form mid–season winning eleven out of fifteen League matches. During this spell Paul spoke about the season and his future with Don Warters *Yorkshire Evening Post*:

We are now all looking forward to games. No sooner is one match over than talk moves on to the next game. Whether I'll realise when the time comes to stop playing or whether I shall

Leeds United, 1977/78. From left to right, back row: Hankin, Harris, Cherry (captain), McQueen, Harvey, Stewart, Clarke, Jordan, Currie, Reaney. Front row: Hampton, McNiven, Graham, Lorimer, E. Gray, Stevenson, Madeley, F. Gray.

MEET THE TEAM

Paul Madeley

... who is set to make his 600th appearance for us during Christmas at Wolves.

It is strange how things work out in football. Here I am on the brink of my 600th appearance in the Leeds United first team and hopefully playing against Manchester City this afternoon — the team we were playing when it all started for me with Leeds back in our Second Division championship winning season of 1963-64.

I was 19 at the time. We won 1-0, I think Don Weston scored our goal and in the City side facing me and also making his debut was Glyn Pardoe. I got my chance because Big Jack was injured and Freddie Goodwin had broken a leg the previous week at Cardiff, since then so much has happened.

I've played every outfield position for Leeds, worn every shirt, seen happy times, sad times, good days, bad days and now I have settled down in one of the central defensive roles I am still enjoying my game and see no reason why I should not play on a few more seasons yet.

The hope is that my move into a permanent place at the back will extend my career with Leeds and things seem to be working well. My days in midfield with John Giles and Billy Bremner have been my most enjoyable but though I am no longer as involved in the game as I was in midfield I find real fulfilment in my defensive job. It is not as physically demanding, you get far more breathers and after all you don't find many players of my age playing anywhere else but at the back. I've always liked to train hard, I've been lucky enough to be a bit pacy and I don't think I've lost that — and that can be important because you can get exposed at the back.

They ask me will I know when the time comes to pack it in — well I think that is difficult to say. I suppose you must get some feelings about it when you really start to struggle. But look at John Giles. They said he was just about finished when he had a run of injuries a few years back but he got over them and he is still playing today. In my case I don't know whether I shall know or I shall be told. I'm sure it helps me to be with a successful team, it keeps driving you on but when it is all over I have no desire to be involved in coaching and I wouldn't fancy being a manager — that side of the game does not appeal to me.

I suppose I'll work in the family wallpaper business. I'm very fortunate to have that to fall back on. In the meantime things seem to be happening again for us here at Leeds. I think we have a very good chance of doing something this time now: that we have improved over the past six or seven matches. It all seems to have happened since Brian Flynn arrived, he seems to have injected us with something that is working out well for Leeds. We are looking less like giving things away — and we have always been capable of scoring goals. There was the time when we were giving too much away but the last four or five games things have tightened up and that is how to get somewhere rather than being an entertaining middle of the table team. Our pool is a little larger now, too and there is some very healthy competition for places — it all keeps everyone on his toes.

If the chance comes I'll be out to give the team what they regard as a Christmas present by adding to my 20-odd goals tally. I seem to pick up goals at this time of year though I missed out last Christmas. My last was Christmas of 75 — funnily enough against Manchester City.

In Focus

Name: PAUL EDWARD MADELEY
Wife's Name: ANN
Children: JASON (7), NICHOLAS (4)
Birthday: 20th SEPTEMBER
Height, Weight: 6 ft., 12 st. 9 lb.
Hobbies: TENNIS, SNOOKER
Favourite Team (after Leeds): LIVERPOOL
Favourite Player: KEVIN KEEGAN
Favourite TV Star: RICHARD BRIERS
Favourite TV Programme: THE GOOD LIFE
Favourite Film Star: PAUL NEWMAN
Favourite Film: JAWS
Favourite Singer: ROD STEWART
Favourite Song: MAGGIE MAY
Favourite Food: STEAK
Favourite Drink: COFFEE
Favourite Holiday Resort: DEVON AND CORNWALL
Favourite Car: MERCEDES
Own Car: VOLVO
Ambition: TO WIN ANOTHER LEAGUE CHAMPIONSHIP WITH LEEDS
Pet Hate: SEEING THE BALL HIT THE BACK OF OUR NET
Best Match: WINNING THE CENTENARY CUP FINAL
Worst Match: LOSING TO SUNDERLAND IN THE CUP FINAL THE FOLLOWING YEAR
Forecasts (from two):
League Champions:
LEEDS UNITED OR NOTTS. FOREST
F.A. Cup Winners:
LEEDS UNITED OR W.B.A.

Everything you wanted to know about Paul is revealed!

have to be told, I can't say, but at the moment I'm enjoying my football as much as ever. Nothing I've experienced this season has indicated that time is approaching. I'm quite content to carry on playing and fully intend turning up for pre-season training next season.

Further inconsistency saw Leeds eventually finish ninth, and there was no FA Cup run to console supporters. In fact, a tense third-round clash with Manchester City at Elland Road saw fans invade the pitch in an attempt to get the match abandoned with Leeds losing, and as tempers flared David Harvey and Gordon McQueen had to be separated after exchanging punches. Leeds lost the game 2-1. Within a few weeks both McQueen and Joe Jordan had departed to Manchester United, much to the anger of supporters. The League Cup however offered an opportunity of a cup final appearance, until Leeds met Nottingham Forest at the semi-final stage. Managing Forest was former manager Brian Clough.

Forest were hitting their peak under Clough and he unearthed some great players. One in particular was their left-winger John Robertson who was fast but unorthodox, and everything seemed to stem through him. Though right footed, when I played right-back he twisted me inside out. They overpowered us in both legs, but I was still really upset to miss out on another Wembley final following our 7-3 aggregate defeat.

LEEDS UNITED

NOTTINGHAM FOREST

FOOTBALL LEAGUE CUP SEMI-FINAL—1st LEG
WEDNESDAY, 8th FEBRUARY, 1978
Official Match Programme 15p

Forest end Leeds' Wembley dreams in the opening leg.

The likes of Brian Flynn, Ray Hankin and Arthur Graham had joined Tony Currie in the side as the 'new Leeds' began to take shape. Although not in the same class as previous stars, they were good players in their own right. However, comparing them to some of the best players ever at Elland Road, and in some cases the best the game had ever seen, was unfair. It placed tremendous pressure on them. Tony for example was immensely gifted, but if he'd been at the club a few years earlier he would not have got in the side. How could he replace Billy Bremner or John Giles? In the circumstances Tony did really well, but losing Joe and Gordon was a tremendous blow because they offered the team so much in attack and defence, but they wanted to move on.

Naturally the atmosphere in the dressing room had changed, but there was still plenty of banter. Brian Flynn in particular was a real bubbly character; very hard working and conscientious. Before a game he was the one who used to go round everyone firing them up before we left the dressing room. He was great to have in the side.

During the 1978/79 close-season legendary Celtic manager Jock Stein replaced Jimmy Armfield as manager, but his stay would only last 44 days. An inconsistent start brought only four wins in the opening fifteen games, including home defeats against both Tottenham and Arsenal. After Stein's replacement, former Burnley boss Jimmy Adamson had settled, results picked up and to Adamson's credit, he guided the team to a place in Europe once again when they finished fifth in the league. The key was a sixteen-game unbeaten run, which included ten victories. Agonisingly though the team missed out on a Wembley cup final.

Although Jimmy had consolidated the team, a lack of silverware resulted in the board appointing a new manager. Duncan McKenzie once quipped about Jimmy, that the 'manager's indecision is final!' This was a bit unfair because in extremely difficult circumstances he did a fine job and it's difficult to see how anyone could have done a better job. Jimmy's last signing was Paul Hart, who I would partner in central defence.

Paul clears this Tottenham attack, but Leeds lose 2-1.

When Jock Stein arrived as manager, I thought he'd be really good. He'd been very friendly with Don and used to talk on the telephone a lot. Don had a lot of time for him. Jock had a great track record with Celtic so it was disappointing, though understandable, when he accepted the Scotland job. Jimmy Adamson was a bit of a father figure because his first-team coach David Merrington spent much more time with us, yet we had a fine season.

Tony Currie had been sensational in the campaign and scored some wonderful goals. One particularly memorable strike was against Southampton in a League clash at Elland Road when he curled in a shot from 25 yards in front of the Kop from open play before blowing kisses to the crowd. He may have been flamboyant and a crowd pleaser, but he also had enormous ability. I was behind the flight of the ball, and I recall thinking how does he do that? The same game I scored my final goal for Leeds, but it wasn't quite as spectacular!

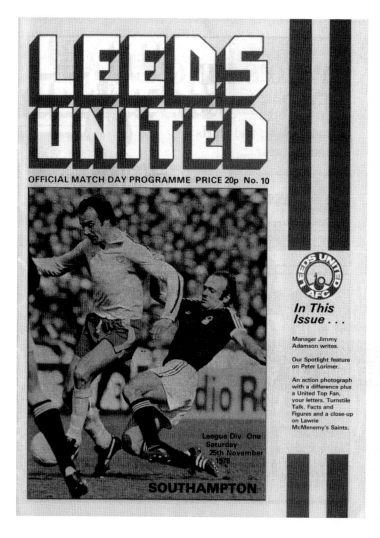

Leeds thump the Saints 4-0, a match when Paul grabbed his last goal for the club ... number 34.

Although we qualified for Europe we missed out for the second year running on a trip to Wembley in the League Cup when we lost in the semi-finals again, this time to Southampton. It was so disappointing because we'd built up a two-goal lead in the first leg at Elland Road before they came back to draw 2-2. One goal in the return was sufficient to eliminate us 3-2 on aggregate. We were all down, and I recall Paul Hart being particularly upset. We were so close to a Wembley final, which was such a big ambition for footballers.

As the decade came to an end, injuries were affecting Paul more and more and Leeds' European journey lasted just two rounds. University Craiova won comfortably 4-0 on aggregate, and Leeds' form was generally inconsistent. Leeds ended the 1979/80 campaign in eleventh place, placing Adamson's job on the line.

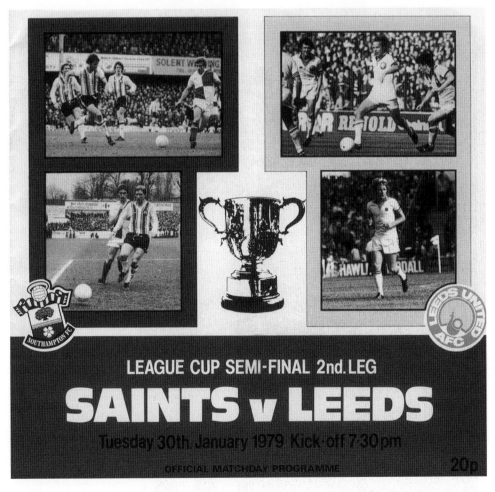

Southampton end Paul's last chance of a Wembley final with a 3-2 aggregate win.

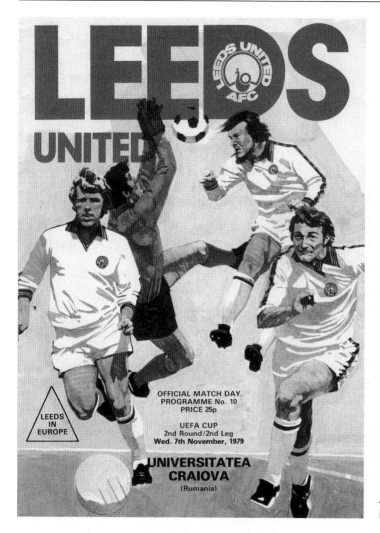

OFFICIAL MATCH DAY
PROGRAMME No. 10
PRICE 25p

UEFA CUP
2nd Round/2nd Leg
Wed. 7th November, 1979

UNIVERSITATEA
CRAIOVA
(Rumania)

LEEDS
IN
EUROPE

A final fling in Europe
is soon extinguished.

When Leeds won just one match in the opening two months of the 1980/81 season Adamson was dismissed. The board turned to former favourite Allan Clarke to revive the club's fortunes. Leeds clawed their way to safety, but for Paul Madeley the end of the road had come. Making just eight appearances during the season Paul brought his 19-year career to a halt against Arsenal on 8 November 1980 at Elland Road.

Following the match, statisticians were finally able to complete a remarkable analysis on the number of times that Paul had worn each shirt for Leeds since making his debut on 11 January 1964. Playing 712 games (plus 13 as a substitute) in all competitions, Paul Madeley's final shirt breakdown stood as follows: No 2 shirt – 76 games, No 3 – 68, No 4 – 25, No 5 – 121, No 6 – 172, No 7 – 15, No 8 – 50, No 9 – 30, No 10 – 21, No 11 – 134 and No 12 – 13. In the process, Paul scored 34 goals.

IN YOUR MATCH PROGRAMME TODAY:
Eddie Gray in Colour
Paul Madeley's big moment . . . see the
Soccer Scene feature
A look at Leeds' Likely Lads
A-Z of Leeds . . . Baker, Bremner and Buckley
A first statistical look at the new season
Leeds — Leicester Match Facts — games that
usually mean goals!

FOOTBALL LEAGUE DIVISION ONE
Saturday 30th August 1980
LEICESTER CITY

700 up! Paul joins Billy Bremner, Jack Charlton, Paul Reaney and Norman Hunter to achieve the feat for Leeds United.

Speaking to the *Yorkshire Evening Post*, thirty-six-year-old Paul said:

I am a realist, no one can go on forever and I will be retiring at the end of the season. The trouble began just before Christmas. It is the knee, which I had a cartilage removed from early in my playing career. Apparently it is an arthritic condition and it will be a struggle for me to play with unless I have an operation. That would mean three to four months out to recover sufficiently to play professional football. Frankly, it does not really seem worthwhile. I'm not

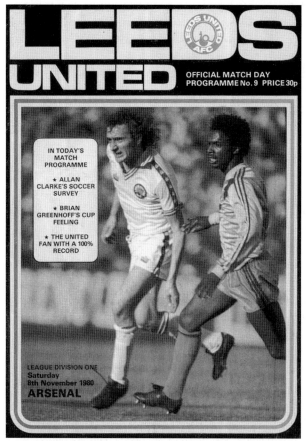

Above: Leeds United, 1980/81. From left to right, back row: Madeley, Stevenson, Hart, Lukic, Arins, Firm, Parlane. Middle row: Thomas, Hamson, Connor, Sabella, Adamson (manager), Curtis, Gray, Dickinson, Entwhistle. Front row: Graham, Hird, Chandler, Cherry (captain), Flynn, Harris, Hampton, Burke.

Left: The final bow ... Paul makes his last first-team appearance for the club.

in the first team and at my age I can hardly figure prominently in the manager's planning for the future. I have been fortunate in my career, I happened to be in the right place at the right time with Leeds and I have enjoyed a terrific amount of involvement. Perhaps we did not lift as many trophies as we might have done, but they were very good years. I shall go out with a treasure store of memories of the greatest post-war team in English football.

Journalists were full of praise for the Leeds legend.

Derek Wallis, *Daily Mirror*: 'My heart sank a little with the news that Paul Madeley is to retire, because in an age when players are so often accused of abusing the laws he remained a footballer who always commanded respect. I cannot recall seeing him commit an offence calculated to ignite trouble or use his considerable height and weight with deliberate intent to foul. He grew up in an era when Leeds United were often accused of underhand and cynical methods, yet Madeley remained a player who seldom put a foot or a word out of place. Throughout his career he has been a model professional, reliable, consistent, dignified and though he remained largely a defender, I always felt that had he been let loose in midfield he might have made an even greater impact on world football.'

Barry Foster, *Yorkshire Post*: 'Even a Rolls-Royce comes to the end of the line eventually ... though fewer owners can have had better service out of their vehicle than Leeds United have out of Paul Madeley. A lot of miles have been covered since the Beeston, Leeds boy joined the club's groundstaff, in January 1962 from Farsley Celtic, but then Rolls are built to give the finest service.'

Ronald Crowther, *Daily* Mail: 'Paul Madeley with his graceful motion, silken skill, placid temperament and freedom from trouble has represented all that is best in the British game. His relaxed strength caused him to be compared so many times with Franz Beckenbauer. The man who has made a success of everything he has done will turn his attention to business.'

Even though I'd played a lot in 1978/79, by 1980/81 I knew it would be my last season with the club. I had a knee problem and a lot of back trouble. At one stage I was seeing a chiropractor every day to enable me to play on a Saturday, which I realised could not continue indefinitely. Eventually I announced that I'd be retiring. Allan Clarke was by now my manager, but I really didn't work under him. Because of the injury problems I only made a few appearances. I helped out with reserve-team training, but it was only temporary. Coaching was not for me.

My last game for Leeds was against Arsenal, we lost 5-0. In their team, Liam Brady shone. I remember once at Highbury showing Liam the inside to avoid him going down the wing. He came across me and bent a left-footer straight into the top corner. There was nothing wrong with what I did; it was simply a tremendous strike. He was a special player.

I'd had a great career, but it was time to bow out. Looking back, my ambition when I joined the club was simply to make the first team. If anyone had said to me at 17 that I'd win six major trophies and play for England on 24 occasions, I'd have said, that'll do for me.

During my era the strength across all the clubs was incredible; everywhere we played there were class players. Often our best performances were reserved for League matches, but even

Happy Memories,
December 1991.

though we came runners-up five times I don't think we could have done much more. We were by far the most consistent team around, and between 1968 and 1974 won more honours than any other team in England, which is often forgotten. Teams had so much respect for us and we became regarded as the team to beat. Every game we played was like a cup final and if a team beat Leeds it was their 'result of the season' and a feather in their cap, which says it all.

For a decade our consistency was incredible. Never finishing outside the top four we reached four FA Cup finals, a League Cup final and five European finals; no other team could match us. Every Leeds team since has been judged against our records, which is a tremendous accolade. Of course it would have been great to win more, but it wasn't to be. During Don's tenure I wonder how many League clubs would have swapped a decade of mediocrity for just one of our seasons. When you think of the humble surroundings at the club when I arrived in 1962, it's astonishing what he achieved.

Over the years I've attended a number of events and it's very gratifying to witness the genuine warmth Leeds fans feel for the team that Don built. Its always nostalgic and it does take you back when you see all the programmes and memorabilia that supporters want signing.

I doubt today's game will produce a group of players that play together for a decade as we did, which is sad in many ways.

I've always felt that being in the right place at the right time is something that happens to people throughout life. I was lucky because I was part of Don Revie's crop of young players at just the right time. The team gets together from time to time, which is very enjoyable and I have so many fantastic memories of my playing career.

After retiring as a player I invested in a sports shop before the family home décor business was sold in December 1987. Today, I'm able to devote my time to my wife Ann and our two sons. I've been incredibly fortunate.

Lucky man! Ann at home with the Nick and Jason.

SUPER LEEDS

By Paul Madeley

Don Revie was the man – who realised a dream
He put together 'Super Leeds' – the finest-ever team
This team of stars from yesteryear – can match against the rest
If you analyse them one by one – they really were the best

First and most importantly – there was strength at the back
This rock of solidarity – was known as Big Jack
Always last onto the pitch – the big man was a star
But when the game was over – he'd be first into the bar!

I really have to say – it was quite a thrill
To play for Leeds United – alongside Captain Bill
Inspirational and tenacious – with an accent tartan red
If only I could have understood – a single word he said!

They didn't call him Sniffer – because he had a cold
But Allan sniffed out chances – that were worth their weight in gold
A player of many talents – a poacher supreme
Goals galore and lots, lots more – from a scoring machine

Mick Jones was always on the move – he gave defenders hell
The very best in the air – he timed his jumps so well
His headers were so accurate – and I've heard it said
When practising a penalty – he took one with his head!

What good business it was for Leeds – on that special day
Don Revie used persuasion – to sign up Eddie Gray
He'd close control, style and pace – no one could ever quibble
Cast your mind back 30 years – to Burnley and that dribble!

Gary Sprake kept his goal – with natural ability
Like all good 'keepers he was blessed – with lots of agility
Good saves were made, high and low – mistakes were just a few
All this from age eighteen – and so good-looking too!

Super Leeds, August 1969. From left to right: Lorimer, Charlton, Clarke, Jones, Gray, Madeley, Cooper, Hunter, Giles, Reaney, Sprake, Bremner.

Attacking full-backs come and go – but none like Terry Cooper
His dazzling displays down the wing – were absolutely super
And it came as no surprise – to those of us that knew him
If he couldn't get around his man – he would go straight through him!

'Hotshot Lorimer' – was the chant throughout the nation
The 'keeper stood between the posts – in fear and trepidation
Up stepped Peter – to blast the ball away
It would have gone in orbit – but the net got in the way!

A goal line clearance guaranteed – at least one every game
Super fit and oh so quick – was Paul Reaney's claim to fame
Man to man marking was his thing – forget about the rest
The only man throughout the league – to tie down Georgie Best

The fans all marvelled at his skill – they came from miles and miles
The sweetest striker of the ball – 'The General' Johnny Giles
Pinpoint passes – all over the park
Left foot or right foot – finding their mark

In those glory days gone by – it was something to be seen
To witness Norman Hunter's –crunch and smile routine
As the striker lay prostrate – he would just back away
'Sorry Ref' Norman said – 'I just mistimed that one today!'

Well that's eleven accounted for – but I must make room for me
After playing seven hundred games – I trust you will agree
For utility men are not required – in the modern game
With subs aplenty on the bench – to cover those when lame

THE LADS OF LEEDS

During two decades Paul Madeley played with many footballers at Leeds United. Many became legends at the club; others gave everything as the club entered a transitional phase. It's impossible to mention everybody but here are Paul's reminiscences about 35 of his teammates at Leeds United.

Mick Bates was a terrific squad member who deputised for Billy and John over a number of years. Don Revie's man-management skills were essential in keeping a player of his quality satisfied, because Mick would undoubtedly have been a regular elsewhere. Joining at the same time as Eddie Gray, someone once asked him if he would have liked Eddie's ability, Mick told them he was satisfied with his own ability, which summed him up. A story he told me also illustrated his philosophy. Against Manchester United when he was due to play, Mick walked past Bobby Charlton, Denis Law and George Best in the corridor and felt a little apprehensive. He then walked into our dressing room and saw Billy, Big Jack and Norman ... Mick thought we'll murder this lot today! He could not have had that feeling at many other clubs. His role was essential as we challenged for trophies each season.

Rod Belfitt was an old-fashioned style centre forward. Although he lacked a bit of pace, Rod was a good finisher. We started as apprentices around the same time and Rod could put the ball away. Don struggled for some time to find the right partnership in attack and changed the strikers around, which must have been frustrating for Rod to just come in for the odd game. After Don teamed up Mick and Allan, Rod moved on to Ipswich Town and Everton where he found some success. Nevertheless, Rod contributed to our early successes and was a member of the squads that won the League Cup and Fairs Cup in 1968.

Willie Bell was very fit and powerful in the air, although he lacked a bit of finesse at times. Willie was a regular in the side when I first broke into the team. His experience was invaluable for the younger players who were just making their way in the game. A Scottish international, Willie eventually lost his place to Terry Cooper, by which time he had been a fine servant to Leeds for many years.

Billy Bremner was some player, an inspiration and a true leader in every sense of the word. He could never have been just an also ran, no matter who he played for when he came south from Scotland. Billy had such an influence on the side with his incredible will to win stamped all over him. Of course he had a fiery temperament, but he was so competitive and desperate to win every game. I've never known anyone with such a fierce determination to succeed. Billy was also so naturally fit. Whenever he came back from injury, which was not that often, it didn't take him long to regain his fitness. He just slotted straight back in … charging about, getting tackles in and causing havoc for our opponents. In midfield, Billy would make great runs to create opportunities for goals, whereas John Giles concentrated on defence-splitting passes; they were the perfect partnership. Billy also scored so many important goals in crucial matches. He was an incredible player and deservedly won the Footballer of the Year award in 1970. Not only was he captain of Leeds but also Scotland and of course led them in the 1974 World Cup finals. When Billy died the whole of football mourned the loss of one of the world's great players. Even today I find it hard to believe he has gone and he is sorely missed. Billy was probably the greatest player I played with during my career.

Jack Charlton was a sensational player for Leeds United. Big Jack was just Big Jack. He wasn't the best of trainers but come match day he was awesome. He was so dependable when you needed him to be. He never missed a volley or header, and the bigger the occasion the better he performed. Jack never let the side down and he scored an incredible number of goals for us from set pieces. His influence over the years was incredible. I played with him in central defence and he was terrific. Jack won everything in the game, and of course was a member of England's World Cup team in 1966 when he was immense. For Leeds he was so reliable, and a real stalwart of the side. His form was recognised in 1967 when he won the prestigious Footballer of the Year award. Jack was always going to move into management and enjoyed success at a number of clubs, especially Middlesborough and the Republic of Ireland.

Trevor Cherry was a really solid defender, he also played in midfield when required and just got on with the job. After coming in for Terry Cooper, Trevor became a great asset to Leeds and we eventually partnered each other in central defence towards the end of my career. Trevor was extremely conscientious about training and was probably the best tackler apart from Norman Hunter at the club. He also scored a number of vital goals, which amazed me because he was in defence most of the time. One against Manchester City in the FA Cup was particularly memorable, and of course he nearly scored in the Cup Final against Sunderland. Everyone remembers Jim Montomery's wonder save from Peter, but it was Trevor's flying header, which the 'keeper somehow saved that rebounded out for Peter's chance. Trevor, who played for England on many occasions and captained the national team, was a great servant to Leeds and went on to lead the side for a number of years.

Allan Clarke was deadly in front of goal and a super finisher. He also enjoyed the tussle of playing in attack! Scoring was so natural to Allan, no matter the conditions. I recall an FA Cup clash against Swindon Town when the pitch was wet and slippery, yet when he got through he had the foresight after rounding the 'keeper, to find the time before cutting back again and making sure with his right foot. It was all so effortless, he was by far the most clinical striker I played with. Allan also scored a number of vital goals, his winner in the '72 Cup Final being particularly special. When he arrived it was brilliant, because we finally had someone who could regularly finish off all the hard work we were putting in. An England international, he coolly scored a penalty on his debut in the 1970 World Cup finals.

Bobby Collins was a tough player and a tremendous influence on the side, especially for the younger players. His signing demonstrated how shrewd Don Revie was because he really kick-started the club in the right direction. During his years at Leeds he was superb because we needed an old head around to dictate things. His experience proved invaluable. Bobby's influence wasn't just in matches though: in training he led by example, and taught me a thing or two on what he expected from me on the pitch! A regular for Scotland during his days with Celtic in the 1950s, Bobby's form was such he earned a recall to the national team. He also won the Footballer of the Year award at the end of our debut Division One campaign in 1964/65. Bobby was one of the best-ever signings for Leeds United.

Terry Cooper converted from being a left-winger to left-back where he became world class. A super tackler, Terry was exceptional going forward when he used to link with Eddie Gray to support the attack. Of course, no one will ever forget his goal against Arsenal in the League Cup final. It was such an important strike, because we'd been runners-up a number of times. At last we were winners. It was a tragedy when he broke his leg in '72, as he was at his peak. Nevertheless, Terry was a great player for Leeds United. An England international, he was sensational in the 1970 World Cup finals when he was acknowledged as being the best in his position in the world.

Tony Currie was an extremely talented player and tremendously skilful. Tony was also immensely strong and had a great ability to shield the ball. When you tried to get near him, his arms would act like vices. You thought it was just for balance but it wasn't, it was like a protective case; you could not get near him. He also scored some fabulous goals, one against Southampton being particularly memorable. Tony was an England international when he arrived at Leeds, and went on to win more caps.

Brian Flynn was really enthusiastic about the game. Before every game he'd go round all the players to encourage them … 'come on, this is it', he was so fired up and ready to go; it was part of his routine. He was a neat player and very nimble about the pitch. A Welsh international, Brian went on to play international football for many years.

John Giles was always thinking about the game, and wanted to play football the way he believed it should be played. During a game he would make his feelings known if you didn't give him the ball when he was in space, and if you made a good pass to someone else, and he felt he was in a better position, he'd give you some glare! John had a great sense of humour. Many times I'd wear a number 11 shirt even though I was playing defensive midfield and as we'd line up in the tunnel, he'd say 'How many times have I told you, stay out on that left-wing!' He was also incredibly hard – if someone kicked him up in the air, they'd know about it later. Speaking with players from my era, a number said they thought John was the hardest player we had. As a footballer though, he'll always be best known as someone who could ping the ball about with either foot and open up any defence, and together with Billy formed the best midfield partnership the club have had. John played and captained the Republic of Ireland for many years.

Arthur Graham could play on either wing. This ability made it very difficult for defenders because he could go either way. A really lively player and extremely dangerous going forward, Arthur scored his share of goals; including a few hat-tricks. Another Scottish international, Arthur was a key member of the side during his time at Leeds and was very popular with supporters.

Eddie Gray was simply 'grace and pace'. It was just such a shame that he was not fit all of the time because he had so much skill on the ball, and when running at defenders was so dangerous; they didn't stand a chance. When Eddie was fit there were few players who could match him, and it does make you wonder what he might have achieved. The thing about Eddie, apart from his terrific ability, was his close control of the ball. He would very rarely knock the ball a few yards in front of a defender and catch him with pace. When he was in possession, the ball was always close to his feet. Although naturally left-footed, most players would have been proud of his control on his right, which was a nightmare for any defender. I faced him on many occasions in training and had nothing but respect for him. I always gave myself as much room as possible, it didn't do me much good though! But for injury, Eddie would have played for Scotland on many more occasions.

Frank Gray was exceptionally skilful and had electric pace, which didn't always show itself. Following his brother Eddie could not have been easy, but such was his skill he made a name for himself and was a fine servant for Leeds, playing at left-back and in midfield with distinction for a number of years. He eventually had a spell at Nottingham Forest where he enhanced his reputation before coming back to Leeds for a second spell. A Scottish international for many years, Frank represented Scotland in two World Cup finals and could hold his own against the best players around.

Jimmy Greenhoff had a lot of ability, but never made it at Leeds. He certainly had the skill and technique but for some reason didn't achieve the breakthrough that his talent warranted. Jimmy was an apprentice when I arrived at Leeds and went on to play in the League Cup-winning team. On his day he scored some super goals, and I was pleased to see him find success at other clubs.

Ray Hankin came into the side towards the end of my career and was another striker who could unnerve defences. Strong, powerful and a leader of the line, Ray was well-built and would put himself about. A handful for defences, Ray was hard to mark because of his strength and heading ability. For a spell he was Leeds' top scorer and was a real asset to the team.

Carl Harris was exceptionally quick and could unlock any defence, but he suffered from inconsistency. However, on his day he was unstoppable, showed terrific pace and could rifle in a terrific shot. I still recall one strike at Middlesborough – it was a fantastic goal. Carl broke into the Leeds side in the mid-1970s but never quite reached his potential, although he went on to represent Wales on many occasions.

Paul Hart was a really solid player and strong in the air. He was also fiercely loyal. I recall getting an elbow at Stoke from Lee Chapman and ending up in hospital. Paul spent the rest of the game trying to kick Lee up in the air! With Paul being very determined and immensely strong in the air, as with Jack and Gordon, I adopted a sweeper role because I could still run a bit. He was a pleasure to partner and I enjoyed playing alongside him. Paul gave everything in every game and became a great servant to the club during a difficult era.

David Harvey got better over the years as his confidence grew. Steady and calm, David may not have been as flamboyant as Gary but he was less likely to let you down. David was incredibly patient waiting for his opportunity but grabbed it when it came. Over the years he made some incredible saves, one at Derby that was destined for the top corner was particularly memorable. A Scottish international, David was voted the best 'keeper at the 1974 World Cup finals.

Terry Hibbitt was another player who was very skilful, but with so many great players at the club it was very hard for him to break through, which must have been frustrating. Terry was a member of the Fairs Cup-winning side in 1968, but eventually moved on to Newcastle United where he played regularly in their first team and got the recognition his skill deserved. Tragically, he died a few years ago.

Kevin Hird was a very capable attacking full-back for Leeds when he joined the club towards the end of my career. Although I only played with him for a short while, it was clear how dedicated he was and he went on to serve Leeds during a difficult period in the club's history. Kevin also played in midfield for Leeds and became the regular penalty taker at one stage. An honest, hard-working player, Kevin always gave his best in every game.

Norman Hunter was my favourite player that I played with. He was always encouraging, made the tackles and led by example. Norman never dwelt on the ball to show how good he was: he would win the ball and move it on. Norman was so reliable, although on occasion he could get a little rattled, as happened against Derby when he got sent off along with Francis Lee, who he felt aggrieved with over a penalty incident earlier in the game. Similarly, Norman may not have been the quickest player, but what a tackler. Okay, he occasionally mistimed some challenges and hoofed an opponent up in the air, but never with malice. He would just let an opponent know he was around! Even in training he'd come in and rattle you to get the ball. I was glad he was my team-mate! For England, but for Booby Moore, he would have won many more caps than he did and, as everyone knows, always gave his best.

Albert Johanneson could do things with the ball that was just astonishing; he was such a skilful player. He had a great left foot and was a real crowd favourite. He played in an era when he had to overcome racial prejudice from the stands. It wasn't easy for him but he let his skills do the talking. Albert became the first black player to play in an FA Cup final and paved the way for future South African footballers. Although he sadly died a few years ago, Leeds supporters will never forget how he could mesmerise defenders with his skills as the team made their way in the top-flight.

Mick Jones was a fantastic target man throughout his career at Leeds. He was so good at holding the ball up, and great in the air. Although Mick may not have been the biggest of strikers in comparison to some centre forwards, his timing was such that he could compete with the best centre-backs around. Mick scored his fair share of goals, many of them crucial. I'll never forget his strikes in the 1970 FA Cup final, and of course his goal won the Fairs Cup in 1968. Mick's game though was much more than just scoring goals. He held the ball up to enable other players to support the attack and made countless goals for Allan and Peter. Mick played for England but should have won many more caps.

Joe Jordan was a player of raw talent when he arrived at Leeds from Morton. A teenager at the time, it was obvious he had a lot of potential and for a number of years deputised for Mick and Allan. Joe had pace, strength and was robust. A lot of people compared him to Mick Jones, but whereas Mick had more deft touches and could hold the ball up better, Joe was quicker and more aggressive in his play. Joe was not the type of striker you would class as a natural goalscorer, but he could unsettle any defender and was a fearsome sight when running at opponents. A veteran of three World Cups for Scotland, Joe went on to excel at Manchester United, AC Milan and Verona.

Peter Lorimer was often classed as a striker because of the phenomenal number of goals he scored, but for me he was a right-winger: that's where he played for many years. Later he played in central midfield, but he was most dangerous from the right flank. Peter was a tremendous striker of the ball and had an amazingly powerful shot. When he first arrived from Scotland, I played in a junior game with him. We were told that he had scored hundreds of goals in schoolboy football, he scored two or three that day as well! Even at fifteen, the power in his shot was just incredible. He could rattle the ball so hard – it was unbelievable. Most lads struggled to get power into a strike or pass a long distance, but he would crack shots in from any distance, it was amazing. It's all to do with timing and it was so natural to him. His strike became his trademark and he became known as 'Hotshot' Lorimer. As a winger he was under-estimated due to his shooting ability, but he had great control, awareness, could beat the best of defenders and had wonderful crossing ability. Of course though, it's his goals that he's remem-bered for. If we were under pressure, he'd often get us out of trouble with a goal and with Peter it couldn't be just a tap in. He used to come up with some outrageous volleys from 30 yards, which would bulge the back of the net. Also, at dead ball situations he was invaluable. If he didn't score direct, often we'd score from ricochets. A Scottish international for a number of years, he scored a great goal in the 1974 World Cup finals.

Gordon McQueen had terrific pace, tremendous agility and ability for such a big lad. He was also majestic in the air. I recall him scoring two late goals to clinch a dramatic win over Middlesborough and of course he scored a famous goal against England at Wembley when Scottish supporters destroyed the goals at the end during wild celebrations. I thoroughly enjoyed playing with him at the back-end of my career because I was able to play the sweeper role, dropping off round the back with him being so prolific in the air. He was young and enthusi-astic, so it wasn't that hard to play with him. Naturally, he went on to serve Scotland on many occasions.

Duncan McKenzie was an instant hit at Leeds after he broke into the side. His tricks and unpredictability were his trademark, and fans loved it. Although at times he could be frustrating to play with, there was no denying his skill, and I soon realised that playing a one-two with Duncan did not necessarily mean you would get it back! Nevertheless, Duncan scored a lot of goals for us in his brief spell, many sensational, and brought a lot of entertainment to supporters, which was great because the club was going through a difficult transitional period. In the penalty box he could be a genius. A dangerous striker, Duncan was a maverick and an entertainer.

Mike O'Grady and I played against each other as schoolboys. Mike was very direct and two-footed, a real schoolboy star. Whilst at Leeds, injury restricted his appearances, but when fit he scored some wonderful goals and was awesome going forward. He made his name at Huddersfield Town before coming to Leeds and his form was such, especially during our first Championship season, that he added to his England caps.

Alan Peacock was a bit past his best when he arrived at Leeds United because he had expe-rienced a lot of knee trouble. Despite this however, he was so powerful in the air and caused a lot of problems for defenders. At the time he was someone we looked up to. Some people felt we actually looked alike when I partnered him in attack! Alan was a key figure in our promotion-winning team, and his form was such that he got a recall into the England side during his spell at the club.

Paul Reaney was probably the fittest player I played with. He was super fit, like a machine, and was by far the best man-marker we had. George Best never relished playing against him, and I recall him giving Don Rogers a torrid time in an FA Cup clash against Swindon Town. Paul was also brilliant at recovering if someone had a head start on him, and of course was famous for his goal-line clearances. I lost count of the number he made, but arguably his most crucial was in the 1972 FA Cup final against Arsenal from Alan Ball's half-volley. Paul was a shade unfortunate to only win a handful of England caps.

Gary Sprake was a stylish goalkeeper who could make incredible saves. On his day he was superb, but he did lose concentration at times. Everyone remembers his errors, which always seemed to be televised and cost us dearly. I'll remember him though for the days when he was unbeatable, his finest hour without doubt coming at the Nep Stadium against Ferencvaros when we clinched the Fairs Cup for the first time. He was outstanding and won us the cup that evening. Gary represented Wales on many occasions.

David Stewart was an instinctive goalkeeper and a superb shot stopper. Although not as dominant as some 'keepers in the penalty area, when it came to one-on-one situations or snap shots David was superb. He came into the side for a couple of spells when David Harvey was injured and never let the team down. His performance against Barcelona in the European Cup semi-final in particular was one I will always remember. He was superb that night and helped us reach the final. His form won him international recognition for Scotland.

Terry Yorath was a good utility member of the squad and a very talented footballer who played in a number of positions. Initially a defender, Terry played mainly in midfield but also in attack. In many ways he was at the club at the wrong time because in any other era he'd have got into the side. Terry had his best spell for Leeds in the 1973/74 Championship season, but went on to enjoy spells with Tottenham and Coventry City. He also had the unusual distinction of becoming a regular for his country before his club! Winning many caps for Wales, Terry became one of the few ex-players to also manage his country.

DOMESTIC AND EUROPEAN PLAYING CAREER

SEASON	DIVISION	LEAGUE			F.A. CUP			LEAGUE CUP			EUROPE			CHARITY SHIELD		TOTAL	
		APPS.	GOALS	POSITION	APPS.	GOALS	ROUND	APPS.	GOALS	ROUND	APPS.	GOALS	ROUND / COMP.	APPS.	GOALS	APPS.	GOALS
1963 - 1964	TWO	4	0	1	2	0	4	0	0	4	0	0	-	0	0	6	0
1964 - 1965	ONE	6	0	2	0	0	F	1	0	3	0	0	-	0	0	7	0
1965 - 1966	ONE	9 + 4s	1	2	0	0	4	2	1	3	4	0	S-F*1	0	0	15 + 4s	2
1966 - 1967	ONE	27 + 1s	2	4	4 + 1s	1	S-F	4	0	4	8	1	F*1	0	0	43 + 2s	4
1967 - 1968	ONE	33 + 3s	7	4	3 + 2s	1	S-F	5	0	W	10 + 1s	2	W*1	0	0	51 + 6s	10
1968 - 1969	ONE	31	3	1	2	0	3	2	1	4	7	0	Q-F*1	0	0	42	4
1969 - 1970	ONE	39	0	2	8	0	F	3	1	3	8	0	S-F*2	1	0	59	1
1970 - 1971	ONE	41	5	2	4	0	5	1	0	2	12	1	W*1	0	0	58	6
1971 - 1972	ONE	42	2	2	7	0	W	4	0	3	1	0	1*3	0	0	54	2
1972 - 1973	ONE	34	0	3	8	0	F	4	0	4	6	0	F*4	0	0	52	0
1973 - 1974	ONE	39	2	1	5	0	5	1	0	2	2	0	3*3	0	0	47	2
1974 - 1975	ONE	38	1	9	6	0	6	4 + 1s	0	4	9	0	Fr2	0	0	59 + 1s	1
1975 - 1976	ONE	39	1	5	2	0	4	2	0	3	0	0	-	0	0	43	1
1976 - 1977	ONE	38	0	10	5	0	S-F	1	0	2	0	0	-	0	0	44	0
1977 - 1978	ONE	38	0	9	1	0	3	6	0	S-F	0	0	-	0	0	45	0
1978 - 1979	ONE	39	1	5	3	0	4	7	0	S-F	0	0	-	0	0	49	1
1979 - 1980	ONE	25	0	11	1	0	3	0	0	2	3	0	2*3	0	0	29	0
1980 - 1981	ONE	8	0	9	0	0	3	2	0	2	0	0	-	0	0	8	0
SUMMARY		528 + 8s	25		64 + 3s	2		49 + 1s	3		70 + 1s	4		1	0	712 + 13s	34

*1 = INTER-CITIES FAIRS CUP
*2 = EUROPEAN CUP
*3 = U. E. F. A. CUP
*4 = EUROPEAN CUP WINNERS CUP

DEBUT: MANCHESTER CITY (HOME), DIVISION TWO, 11-Jan-64 (WON 1-0)
LAST GAME: ARSENAL (HOME), DIVISION ONE, 8-Nov-80 (LOST 0-5)

OTHER GAMES (NOT INCLUDED ABOVE)
GLASGOW SELECT XI (HAMPDEN PARK), GLASGOW CHARITY CUP, 10-Aug-66 (DRAW 1 - 1, SHIRT NO.12)
SCOTLAND UNDER-23 (HAMPDEN PARK), CHALLENGE MATCH, 19-May-75 (LOST 2 - 3 & SHIRT NO. 5)
BRADFORD CITY (VALLEY PARADE), WEST RIDING SENIOR CUP, 5-Jun-80 (WON 4 - 1, SHIRT NO.6)

CUP FINALS & CHARITY SHIELD APPEARANCES

NO.	SHIRT NUMBER	DATE	COMPETITION	OPPOSITION	VENUE	SCORE	ATTENDANCE
1	9	02-Mar-68	LEAGUE CUP	ARSENAL	WEMBLEY, LONDON	WON 1 - 0	97,887
2	10	07-Aug-68	INTER-CITIES FAIRS CUP (1ST. LEG)	FERENCVAROS	ELLAND ROAD, LEEDS	WON 1 - 0	25,268
3	10	11-Sep-68	INTER-CITIES FAIRS CUP (2ND. LEG)	FERENCVAROS	NEP STADIUM, BUDAPEST	DRAW 0 - 0	76,000
4	7	02-Aug-69	CHARITY SHIELD	MANCHESTER CITY	ELLAND ROAD, LEEDS	WON 2 - 1	39,835
5	2	11-Apr-70	F. A. CUP	CHELSEA	WEMBLEY, LONDON	DRAW 2 - 2	100,000
6	2	29-Apr-70	F. A. CUP	CHELSEA	OLD TRAFFORD, MANCHESTER	LOST 1 - 2	62,078
7	11	28-May-71	INTER-CITIES FAIRS CUP (1ST. LEG)	JUVENTUS	STADIO COMMUNALE, TURIN	DRAW 2 - 2	45,000
8	11	02-Jun-71	INTER-CITIES FAIRS CUP (2ND. LEG)	JUVENTUS	ELLAND ROAD, LEEDS	DRAW 1 - 1	42,483
9	3	06-May-72	F. A. CUP	ARSENAL	WEMBLEY, LONDON	WON 1 - 0	100,000
10	5	05-May-73	F. A. CUP	SUNDERLAND	WEMBLEY, LONDON	LOST 0 - 1	48,470
11	11	16-May-73	EUROPEAN CUP WINNERS CUP	A. C. MILAN	SALONIKA	LOST 0 - 1	25,000
12	5	28-May-75	EUROPEAN CUP	BAYERN MUNICH	PARC DES PRINCES, PARIS	LOST 0 - 2	48,374

PAUL MADELEY: GOALS FOR LEEDS UNITED

GOAL NOS.	OPPOSITION	VENUE	DATE	COMPETITION	RESULT
1	**LEICESTER CITY**	AWAY	**18-Sep-65**	**DIVISION ONE**	**DRAW 3 - 3**
2	**WEST BROMWICH ALBION**	HOME	**13-Oct-65**	**LEAGUE CUP**	**LOST 2 - 4**
3	MANCHESTER UNITED	HOME	27-Aug-66	DIVISION ONE	WON 3 - 1
4	ARSENAL	HOME	15-Oct-66	DIVISION ONE	WON 3 - 1
5	**DWS AMSTERDAM**	HOME	**26-Oct-66**	**INTER-CITIES FAIRS CUP**	**WON 5 - 1**
6	**WEST BROMWICH ALBION**	HOME	**18-Feb-67**	**F. A. CUP**	**WON 5 - 0**
7	SPORA LUXEMBOURG	AWAY	3-Oct-67	INTER-CITIES FAIRS CUP	WON 9 - 0
8	STOKE CITY	HOME	2-Dec-67	DIVISION ONE	WON 2 - 0
9 & 10	SOUTHAMPTON	HOME	13-Jan-68	DIVISION ONE	WON 5 - 0
11	LEICESTER CITY	AWAY	3-Feb-68	DIVISION ONE	DRAW 2 - 2
12	SHEFFIELD UNITED	HOME	30-Mar-68	F. A. CUP	WON 1 - 0
13	SHEFFIELD UNITED	HOME	6-Apr-68	DIVISION ONE	WON 3 - 0
14	TOTTENHAM HOTSPUR	AWAY	12-Apr-68	DIVISION ONE	LOST 1 - 2
15	WEST BROMWICH ALBION	HOME	20-Apr-68	DIVISION ONE	WON 3 - 1
16	DUNDEE	AWAY	1-May-68	INTER-CITIES FAIRS CUP	DRAW 1 - 1
17	LEICESTER CITY	AWAY	14-Sep-68	DIVISION ONE	DRAW 1 - 1
18	CRYSTAL PALACE	AWAY	16-Oct-66	LEAGUE CUP	LOST 1 - 2
19	COVENTRY CITY	AWAY	16-Nov-68	DIVISION ONE	WON 1 - 0
20	NEWCASTLE UNITED	HOME	26-Dec-68	DIVISION ONE	WON 2 - 1
21	CHELSEA	HOME	24-Sep-69	LEAGUE CUP	DRAW 1 - 1
22	BLACKPOOL	HOME	14-Nov-70	DIVISION ONE	WON 3 - 1
23	STOKE CITY	HOME	18-Nov-70	DIVISION ONE	WON 4 - 1
24	WOLVERHAMPTON WANDERERS	AWAY	21-Nov-70	DIVISION ONE	WON 3 - 2
25	LIVERPOOL	AWAY	5-Dec-70	DIVISION ONE	DRAW 1 - 1
26	WOLVERHAMPTON WANDERERS	HOME	20-Feb-71	DIVISION ONE	WON 3 - 0
27	*JUVENTUS*	*AWAY*	*28-May-71*	*INTER-CITIES FAIRS CUP*	*DRAW 2 - 2*
28	NEWCASTLE UNITED	HOME	1-Sep-71	DIVISION ONE	WON 5 - 1
29	CRYSTAL PALACE	HOME	4-Sep-71	DIVISION ONE	WON 2 - 0
30	ARSENAL	AWAY	28-Aug-73	DIVISION ONE	WON 2 - 1
31	NEWCASTLE UNITED	AWAY	26-Dec-73	DIVISION ONE	WON 1 - 0
32	SHEFFIELD UNITED	AWAY	1-Apr-75	DIVISION ONE	DRAW 1 - 1
33	MANCHESTER CITY	AWAY	26-Dec-75	DIVISION ONE	WON 1 - 0
34	SOUTHAMPTON	HOME	25-Nov-78	DIVISION ONE	WON 4 - 0

THE BOLD ENTRIES SHOW PAUL'S FIRST GOALS FOR LEEDS UNITED IN EACH COMPETITION
THE BOLD AND ITALIC ENTRY SHOWS PAUL'S ONLY CUP FINAL GOAL

PAUL SCORED MORE THAN ONE GOAL IN A GAME ON ONE OCCASION (13-Jan-68)
PAUL SCORED THREE GOALS IN CONSECUTIVE GAMES TWICE (30-Mar to 12-Apr-68 & 14-21 Nov-70)
PAUL SCORED ON BOXING DAY IN 1968, 1973 & 1975

GAMES IN WHICH PAUL WORE EACH SHIRT FOR THE FIRST TIME

SHIRT NO.	OPPOSITION	VENUE	DATE	COMPETITION	RESULT
2	VALENCIA	AWAY	08-Feb-67	INTER-CITIES FAIRS CUP	WON 2 - 0
3	STOKE CITY	AWAY	10-Oct-64	DIVISION ONE	WON 3 - 2
4	ASTON VILLA	HOME	14-Oct-64	LEAGUE CUP	LOST 2 - 3
5	MANCHESTER CITY (DEBUT)	HOME	11-Jan-64	DIVISION TWO	WON 1 - 0
6	STOKE CITY	AWAY	01-Oct-66	DIVISION ONE	DRAW 0 - 0
7	ARSENAL	AWAY	05-Nov-66	DIVISION ONE	WON 1 - 0
8	NEWCASTLE UNITED	HOME	13-Sep-66	LEAGUE CUP	WON 1 - 0
9	CHELSEA	AWAY	12-Feb-66	F. A. CUP	LOST 0 - 1
10	PRESTON NORTH END	HOME	12-Oct-66	LEAGUE CUP	WON 4 - 0
11	CHELSEA	AWAY	20-Mar-68	DIVISION ONE	DRAW 0 - 0
12*	TOTTENHAM HOTSPUR	HOME	15-Sep-65	DIVISION ONE	WON 2 - 0

* THIS IS THE FIRST GAME WHERE PAUL CAME ON AS SUBSTITUTE IN A GAME

INTERNATIONAL PLAYING CAREER

CAP	SHIRT NUMBER	DATE	COMPETITION	OPPOSITION	VENUE	SCORE	ATTENDANCE
1	2	15-May-71	HOME INTERNATIONAL CHAMPIONSHIP	NORTHERN IRELAND	WINDSOR PARK, BELFAST	WON 1 - 0	33,000
2	8	13-Oct-71	EUROPEAN CHAMPIONSHIP QUALIFIER	SWITZERLAND	BASLE	WON 3 - 2	47,877
3	2	10-Nov-71	EUROPEAN CHAMPIONSHIP QUALIFIER	SWITZERLAND	WEMBLEY, LONDON	DRAW 1 - 1	90,423
4	2	01-Dec-71	EUROPEAN CHAMPIONSHIP QUALIFIER	GREECE	PIRAEUS	WON 2 - 0	34,014
5	2	29-Apr-72	EUROPEAN CHAMPIONSHIP QUALIFIER	WEST GERMANY	WEMBLEY, LONDON	LOST 1 - 3	100,000
6	2	13-May-72	EUROPEAN CHAMPIONSHIP QUALIFIER	WEST GERMANY	BERLIN	DRAW 0 - 0	76,200
7	2	20-May-72	HOME INTERNATIONAL CHAMPIONSHIP	WALES	NINIAN PARK, CARDIFF	WON 3 - 0	34,000
8	2	27-May-72	HOME INTERNATIONAL CHAMPIONSHIP	SCOTLAND	HAMPDEN PARK, GLASGOW	WON 1 - 0	119,325
9	5	14-Feb-73	FRIENDLY	SCOTLAND	HAMPDEN PARK, GLASGOW	WON 5 - 0	48,470
10	2	27-May-73	FRIENDLY	CZECHOSLOVAKIA	PRAGUE	DRAW 1 - 1	25,000
11	2	06-Jun-73	WORLD CUP QUALIFIER	POLAND	CHORZOW	LOST 0 - 2	73,714
12	2	10-Jun-73	FRIENDLY	USSR	MOSCOW	WON 2 - 1	85,000
13	2	14-Jun-73	FRIENDLY	ITALY	TURIN	LOST 0 - 2	60,000
14	2	26-Sep-73	FRIENDLY	AUSTRIA	WEMBLEY, LONDON	WON 7 - 0	48,000
15	2	17-Oct-73	WORLD CUP QUALIFIER	POLAND	WEMBLEY, LONDON	DRAW 1 - 1	100,000
16	2	14-Nov-73	FRIENDLY	ITALY	WEMBLEY, LONDON	LOST 0 - 1	88,000
17	2	30-Oct-74	EUROPEAN CHAMPIONSHIP QUALIFIER	CZECHOSLOVAKIA	WEMBLEY, LONDON	WON 3 - 0	83,858
18	2	20-Nov-74	EUROPEAN CHAMPIONSHIP QUALIFIER	PORTUGAL	WEMBLEY, LONDON	DRAW 0 - 0	84,461
19	2	16-Apr-75	EUROPEAN CHAMPIONSHIP QUALIFIER	CYPRUS	WEMBLEY, LONDON	WON 5 - 0	68,245
20	2	30-Oct-75	EUROPEAN CHAMPIONSHIP QUALIFIER	CZECHOSLOVAKIA	BRATISLAVA	LOST 1 - 2	50,651
21	11	19-Nov-75	EUROPEAN CHAMPIONSHIP QUALIFIER	PORTUGAL	LISBON	DRAW 1 - 1	60,000
22	5	13-Jun-76	WORLD CUP QUALIFIER	FINLAND	HELSINKI	WON 4 - 1	24,336
23	3	08-Sep-76	FRIENDLY	REPUBLIC OF IRELAND	WEMBLEY, LONDON	DRAW 1 - 1	51,030
24	6	09-Feb-77	FRIENDLY	HOLLAND	WEMBLEY, LONDON	LOST 0 - 2	90,260

PAUL REPRESENTED THE FOOTBALL LEAGUE AGAINST THE LEAGUE OF IRELAND IN 1969 & WENT ON AN F.A. COMMONWEALTH TOUR TO CANADA IN 1967